A CRAFTER'S BOOK OF
Angels

Deborah Morgenthal

Sterling Publishing Co., Inc.   New York
A Sterling/Lark Book

With love, for my father, James Samuel Morgenthal, a model of intelligence, perseverance, and tolerance; an angel of a dad, who has just turned 80 years young.

Contributing Editors: Holly Boswell and Sheila Geitner Shulz
Art Director: Elaine Thompson
Photography: Richard Babb
Photography Stylist: Jodee Mitchell
Illustrations: Alex James
Production: Elaine Thompson

Library of Congress Cataloging-in-Publication Data
Morgenthal, Deborah.
    A crafter's book of angels / by Deborah Morgenthal.
      p. cm.
    "A Sterling/Lark book."
    Includes index.
    ISBN 0-8069-3156-6
    1. Handicraft.   2. Angels in art.   I. Title.
  TT157.M638   1995
  745.5--dc20   95-6210
                                        CIP

10 9 8 7 6 5 4 3 2 1

A Sterling/Lark Book

Published in 1995 by Sterling Publishing Co., Inc.
  387 Park Avenue South, New York, NY 10016

Produced by Altamont Press, Inc.
  50 College Street, Asheville, NC 28801

© 1995, Altamont Press

Distributed in Canada by Sterling Publishing
  c/o Canadian Manda Group, One Atlantic Ave., Suite 105,
  Toronto, Ontario, Canada M6K 3E7
Distributed in Great Britain and Europe by Cassell PLC
  Wellington House, 125 Strand, London, England WC2R 0BB
Distributed in Australia by Capricorn Link (Australia) Pty Ltd.
  P.O. Box 6651, Baulkham Hills, Business Center, NSW 2153, Australia

Every effort has been made to ensure that all the information in this book is accurate. However, due to differing conditions, tools, and individual skills, the publisher cannot be responsible for any injuries, losses, and other damages which may result from the use of the information in this book.

ISBN 0-8069-3156-6

Printed in Hong Kong.

Contents

Contributing
Designers

SANDRO BOTTICELLI, "MYSTIC NATIVITY," 1444–1510. NATIONAL GALLERY, COURTESY OF E.T. ARCHIVE, LONDON.

Marjorie Ingalls Beaty crafted her first doll over 20 years ago as a gift for her daughter, and still enjoys the good humor that seems to come to life in her creations. She lives in Newbury, Massachusetts.

Virginia Boegli began her experiments with paper mache 35 years ago as a tool for studying form and movement for her paintings. Since then, her pieces have ranged from three-inch chess figures to 10-foot bronze replicas. She lives in Bozeman, Montana.

Lula Chang has, for the past 10 years, happily combined her passion for needlework and her vocation as an illustrator into Wooly Dreams Design in Columbia, Maryland, offering fine, hand-painted needlepoint canvases, cross-stitch charts, and kits.

Susan R. Dilan discovered the beauty of Tarjeteria soon after moving to Puerto Rico in 1985. She soon began to create projects with English instruction in order to promote this craft and her new home to the rest of the world.

Jeanne H. Fallier teaches, hooks, lectures, designs, and writes about hooked rugs from her studio, The Rugging Room, in Westford, Massachusetts. She has been hooking rugs for nearly 40 years.

Pamela S. Forsythe creates dolls from antique fabrics, linens, and laces. Her home business, Parsnips and Old Lace, is located in Raleigh, North Carolina

Trudel Terhune Gifford is a multi-media artist living in Santa Fe, New Mexico, where she creates tin angels and other flying beings that often express her own joy and mischievous humor.

Beverly Gottfried is a homemaker, dental hygienist, wife, and mother of two daughters, living in Asheville, North Carolina.

Marie-Helene Grabman is a member of the Guild of American Papercutters and has won several awards in juried shows. She lives in Charlotte, North Carolina.

Christi Hensley lives in the Blue Ridge Mountains of North Carolina, where she shares her life with her husband, Harry, her children, Cara Beth and Emory, 12 goats, two dogs, and two cats.

Judy Horn sells her cornhusk dolls, wreaths, and arrangements at her shop, The Corn Husk Shoppe, in Weaverville, North Carolina.

Dana Irwin, a designer for a book publishing company, likes to dance, make music, and create art. She lives in Asheville, North Carolina with her dog and two cats.

Jacqueline Janes is a full-time polymer clay artist and instructor who works from her studio, Eggplant, in Tempe, Arizona. As President of the Arizona Polymer Clay Guild, she actively promotes polymer clay as a medium.

Susan Kinney is a papermaker, potter, jeweler, and an interior designer who lives in Asheville, North Carolina.

George Knoll of Leicester, North Carolina, handcrafts a variety of wood products from fine jewelry boxes to rustic lamps made from fallen wood.

Susan Koppi is a special education teacher who turns to fabric and her sewing machine for relaxation and a creative outlet. She lives in Asheville, North Carolina.

Diane Kroll is a homemaker, wife, and mother of five who loves crafts of all types, the more challenging the better. She lives in Arden, North Carolina.

Diane C. Kuebitz, who lives in Salt Lake City, Utah, draws her inspiration from whimsical spirits and numerous nature guides. Her six-year-old son, Edward, often helps her name her designs.

Claudia Lee is a full-time studio papermaker and instructor in Kingsport, Tennessee. Her handmade paper angels are a part of her production line that she sell to shops and galleries.

Dort Lee comes from a long line of artists who all believed in angels. An artist, quilter, and gardener, she lives with her husband and two children on a farm in the North Carolina mountains.

Susan McCarson started sewing figures of animals and people as a hobby. Now she's in business full time, selling her line of angels and nonwinged creatures to craft stores and boutiques. She lives in Swannanoa, North Carolina.

Jan Miles is certified as a Decorative Painter with the City and Guilds of North America. She is currently working as a "have brush will travel" decorative painter in the western North Carolina region. She lives in Waynesville, North Carolina.

Mary Jane Miller and **Valentin Gomez** are full-time studio artists, who utilize decorative painting, woodworking, and a range of other techniques to make beautiful art together. They live half the year in Abingdon, Virginia, and the other half in Mexico.

Martha Mitchell is a designer for commissioned glasswork at Touch of Glass in Asheville, North Carolina.

Dolly Lutz Morris markets her hand-sculpted, one-of-a-kind dolls, angels, and animal figures from her workshops in Saegertown, Pennsylvania. She also teaches paper mache and doll making.

Dolores Muller, a graphic artist by profession, fell in love with wheat weaving in 1978. Since then, she and her husband, Ron, have been weaving many of the patterns of antiquity, as well as creating designs of their own from their studio, Carolina Wheat, in Southern Pines, North Carolina.

Beth Palmer is a painter and decorative artist who specializes in home accessories. She lives in Greensboro, North Carolina.

Mary Parker pursues a career in public sector finance in order to indulge her passion for fabric. She lives in Asheville, North Carolina with her husband and six cats.

Nan and **Bill Parker** are teachers who retired from Florida to Mountain Rest, South Carolina. They enjoy crafting for friends and for shows.

Patti Przybylinski has a new and thriving business, Long Winter Dolls, in her hometown of Ferrisburgh, Vermont.

Elsie Pugh owns a craft supply store with her daughter, Brenda, and enjoys crafts of all kinds. She lives in Asheville, North Carolina.

Catherine Reurs, a former career banker in Europe, is an internationally known needlepoint and cross-stitch designer. Her designs are featured in the book *In Splendid Detail: Needlepoint Art,* and she sells her needlepoint and cross-stitch kits through her business, In Splendid Detail, in Watertown, Massachusetts.

Cathi Rosengren was a cosmetics executive for 15 years prior to opening her shop, "i'm in stitches," in Newburyport, Massachusetts. In her classes, she shares her passion for needlepoint by combining fine, hand-painted canvases with her imaginative use of fibers and stitches.

Maggie Rotman is an artist currently working in fiber. She lives in Asheville, North Carolina.

Pat Schieble, a former research biologist, keeps busy with trompe l'oeil and faux finish work for commercial and residential clients in the southeast. Ideas spill over into painted furniture, jewelry, and clothing design. The common thread is a certain zaniness. She lives in Raleigh, North Carolina.

Tom Schulz is an artist, designer, and builder who lives in Asheville, North Carolina. His work has been exhibited throughout the southeast and is part of many private collections.

George Summers, Jr., a batik artist, teaches batik to teenagers and adults in Boston, Massachusetts. He lives in Summerville, Massachusetts, and indeed, believes in angels.

Jennifer Drake Thomas applies her artistic talents to a range of materials from clay to fiber, and she spends much of her time teaching her skills to her two young daughters. The family lives in Asheville, North Carolina.

Patricia Taylor is a self-taught fiber artist who has sold her work to shops and galleries nationwide. Her bears are close to her heart and can always be found watching over her studio in Winston-Salem, North Carolina.

Terry Taylor creates art for the garden using the pique-assiette medium. He also combines pique-assiette with tramp art carving to make decorative objects for interior spaces. He collects, creates, and carves from his home in Asheville, North Carolina.

Nola Theiss is the author of many needlecraft books and a nationally known teacher of knitting and crochet. She is the founder of New Works, Inc., a company that designs knitwear and translates and edits knitting patterns from different languages. She also owns CottonTale/Mayflower Yarn/Ruby Mills, a distributor of natural and recycled yarn for the knitting industry and the home needlecrafter.

Bonnie Troyer attributes her attraction to folk art crafts to her love for old things. When she is not carving and painting, she is in her yard or working for a nursery and garden center in Fairview, North Carolina.

David Vance, with a degree in seminary, is a self-taught artist. He started out carving people, angels, and animals from wood. Although he is now painting on canvas, he can't entirely leave wood alone. He lives in Asheville, North Carolina.

Don C. Wood teaches stained glass at Western Carolina University in Cullowhee, North Carolina.

Carol Weyrauch teaches art and chairs the art department in a junior high school in Salt Lake City, Utah.

Carol Wilcox Wells drew and painted for years before her passion for beads took over. Now she "paints" with beads, and her work is shown and sold through galleries. She is a nationally known beading instructor, and runs a bead mail order company called Carol Wilcox Wells in Asheville, North Carolina.

Michelle West operates a boutique called Floral Designs by Michelle, in Asheville, North Carolina, where she designs for homes, weddings, and offices.

Lesa Winchester is always trying new things in crafting, when she is not too busy as a housewife and mother of two children in Asheville, North Carolina.

Ellen Zahorec is a mixed media studio artist specializing in handmade paper and collage. Her work has been shown internationally and is part of numerous private and corporate collections. She lives in Cincinnatti, Ohio.

PEAR, FROM A 17TH-CENTURY CUSHION COVER DEPICTING ABRAHAM AND THE ANGELS. VICTORIA & ALBERT MUSEUM, COURTESY OF E. T. ARCHIVE, LONDON.

Introduction

〜

An analysis of the final years of the 20th century will most likely include a remarkable fact: most Americans believe in the existence of angels (*Time* poll, 1993). This belief has generated a veritable seraphim smorgasbord: there are seminars on how to get in touch with your inner angel, college-level courses on the history of angels, whole sections of book stores devoted to books recounting people's encounters with angels, numerous feature films and prime-time television programs with angel themes, a wave of fine art inspired by visions of angels, and the emergence in many cities of boutiques that offer only factory-made and handmade angel gifts and keepsakes.

While this phenomenon may be one of many defining elements of present-day Western culture, the belief in and study of angels, as well as their depiction by artists, is nearly universal, spanning centuries. Writings about angels and artistic renderings of them appear in early Hebrew and Christian traditions, in classical myth and philosophy, and in Zoroastrianism, Hinduism, Buddhism, Taoism, and Islam.

Although their role has differed over time and across cultures, the central idea is shared: angels belong to the world of ethereal beings who serve as intermediaries between the ordinary earthbound life of humans and the transcendent realm of the divine. In the Judaeo-Christian tradition, the word angel comes from the Greek aggelos, which translates the Hebrew mal'akh, both meaning messenger.

Winged messengers appear on fourth century B.C. Greek urns, in ancient Sumerian carvings, Egyptian tombs, and Assyrian reliefs. Paintings of angels by early Christians look like transfigured ancient gods and goddesses. In all these visual renderings, we are able to recognize the angelic, even though their physical natures vary.

GIOVANNI MARTINI, "MUSICAL ANGELS," 733. MUSEO CIVICO UDINE, COURTESY OF E.T. ARCHIVE, LONDON.

In ancient and contemporary times, the image of the angel in art appears to be a creative interplay between traditional religious descriptions, the influences of the particular culture, and the artist's individual perceptions. The angels in this book, both in the Gallery section and among the 75 crafts projects featured, vividly demonstrate that creative interplay.

When I first began work on this book, I was bothered by the notion that I would wind up only with angels of the strictly "saccharin" variety: you know, flowing blond hair, billowing gown, mysterious yet kindly smile, size six waistline. Not that I have reason to doubt that some angels look like that. But for me, a ball-juggling, working mom, three-year-old daughter, husband in nursing school, two dogs, two cats—you get the idea—most days my vision of an angel is more down-to-earth. In fact, when I first saw The Difficult Angel (page 23), my heart sang: "This is what my guardian angel looks like— harried, frazzled, but finally here!"

As you look through this first-of-its-kind book, I'm sure you will find angels that speak to you. The talented designers whose work graces these pages "see" angels that vary in gender, ethnicity, age, and every possible aspect of physical appearance. (Some even walk on four legs.) This marvelous diversity is evidenced in another striking manner: the angels are made from a wide range of materials, using a number of craft techniques. For instance, you'll find angels made of silk, polymer clay, stained glass, and wood that you can sew, hammer, batik, sculpt, and paint. Here, in one book, are projects representing today's most popular craft techniques. We believe this diversity of style, materials, and technique makes this an appealing book you'll enjoy using for years to come. It also, however, makes this a challenging book. Because there is a limit to how many pages a book can run, we could not offer a basic techniques section to address all the techniques these projects utilize. Which means that if you have never used polymer clay and don't know a face cane from a candy cane, you will need to do some homework before you try some of the polymer clay projects. If that's the case, we suggest you look at *Creative Clay Jewelry*, by Leslie Dierks (Sterling/Lark,

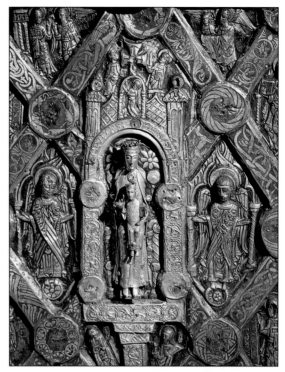

"THE VIRGIN MARY ENTHRONED WITH ANGELS," 1125–1150, ON AN ALTARFRONT FROM LISBJERG NEAR ÅRHUS. NATIONAL MUSEUM OF COPENHAGEN, COURTESY OF E.T. ARCHIVE, LONDON.

STEFANO DA VERONA, "ANGELS PLAYING MUSIC," 1357–1451. CORRER MUSEUM, VENICE, COURTESY OF E.T. ARCHIVE, LONDON.

1994), and work through the basics section. If you are new to sewing, some of the projects may be too complicated for you (others will be perfect). In that case, find a copy of *The Complete Book of Sewing Short Cuts*, by Claire B. Shaeffer (Sterling, 1981), or other comprehensive sewing manuals.

There are three ways you can use this book. If you are accomplished with, say, paper mache, you'll choose the projects that match your ability and taste, and off you'll go. Or, you may decide to use a project as a starting point for making a paper mache angel of your own imagining.

Secondly, if you have always wanted to try stained glass or decorative painting, the book can serve as a catalyst for you to finally learn how. Then, you can come back to those projects you admire and easily follow the instructions.

And finally, if you picked up this book mistakenly thinking it was another exploration of angel encounters, perhaps your guardian angel is trying to encourage you to explore the artist in you. Crafts are no longer something that other people do—they are what you can do. In this era of mass-produced everything, the appeal of carefully making something by hand is very strong. Many people hold to the idea that God is in the details. If that is so, then certainly angels are in the loving nudge ("try it...now!").

If you want to get in touch with your inner angel, or if you simply love anything angelic, I hope you will use this book in the spirit in which it's intended: as a celebration of what we are capable of making with skillful hands and care-full hearts.

ABBOT HANDERSON THAYER, "ANGEL," 1889. COURTESY OF NATIONAL MUSEUM OF AMERICAN ART, WASHINGTON, D.C., ART RESOURCE, NEW YORK, GIFT OF JOHN GELLATLY.

Margaret Agner, "The Guardians II," hand-painted silk quilting, 30" x 40" (77 x 102.5 cm). Photo: Margaret Agner.

Margaret Agner, "Go Tell the People," hand-painted silk quilting, 31" x 13" (33.5 x 79.5 cm). Photo: Margaret Agner.

Dan Reiser, "The Shield," from Art, Lies, and Archaeology series, paper, plaster, and resin casting, 16" x 24" (41 x 61.5 cm).

MARY SHEPPARD BURTON, "THE DANCING ANGEL," TAPESTRY HOOKING ON LINEN WITH ANTIQUE BEADS, 14" (36 CM) HIGH.

THRACE SHIRLEY, "CERAMIC ANGEL," PAINTED CERAMIC, 13-1/2" (34.5 CM) TALL. PHOTO: EWART BALL.

DAVID ARONSON, "ANGELS OF LIGHT, MENORAH," BRONZE, 17" X 17" X 5" (43.5 X 43.5 X 13 CM). COURTESY OF PUCKER GALLERY, BOSTON. PHOTO: VICTORIA FULLERTON.

SARAH KATZ, "WINGED WOMAN III," CERAMIC, 28" (72 CM) HIGH. PHOTO: STEVE BATES.

GEORGE SUMMERS, JR., "ANGEL SLEEPING IN THE HAND OF GOD," BATIK ON COTTON BROADCLOTH, 16" x 16" (41 x 41 CM). PHOTO: RICHARD BABB.

KATY HUTCHINS, "MAY YOU ALWAYS BE PROTECTED," RAKU, 5" x 5" (13 x 13 CM). PHOTO: BILL WICKETT.

MAR GOMAN, "THOUSAND ANGELS," FROM SERIES, MIXED MEDIA, 10" (25.5 CM) AVERAGE HEIGHT. PHOTO: MAR GOMAN.

ALEXANDER ANUFRIEV, "DISCOVERY," OIL ON CANVAS, 16" x 20" (41 x 51 CM). COURTESY OF PUCKER GALLERY, BOSTON.

DAVID VANCE, "WHEN THE ANGELS SING THE BLUES, MY SOUL REJOICES IN SHADES OF INDIGO, PTHALO, AND AQUAMARINE (DETAIL)," SCULPTED AND PAINTED WOOD, 3' (92.5 CM) TALL. PHOTO: RICHARD BABB.

SAMUEL BAK, "ANGELS AND THEIR GUARDIANS," OIL ON CANVAS, 31-7/8" X 39-1/4" (81.75 X 100.5 CM). COURTESY OF PUCKER GALLERY, BOSTON.

ALEXANDER ANUFRIEV, "PROCLAMATION," OIL ON CANVAS, 20" X 24" (51 X 61.5 CM). COURTESY OF PUCKER GALLERY, BOSTON.

MAGGIE RUDY, "SMALL ANGEL," PAPER MACHE, FABRIC, POLYMER CLAY, 8-1/2" (22 CM) HIGH. PHOTO: BILL BACHHUBER.

CAROL DRUMMOND, "SANCTUM," MIXED MEDIA QUILT, 32" x 36" (82 x 92 CM). PHOTO: RICHARD DRUMMOND.

G. CAROL BOMER, "LOOK HOMEWARD, ANGEL," WATERCOLOR ON PAPER, 22" x 30" (56.5 x 77 CM).

GEORGE SUMMERS, JR., "GUARDIAN ANGEL," BATIK ON COTTON BROADCLOTH, 16" x 16" (41 x 41 CM). PHOTO: RICHARD BABB.

ANTONETTE CELY, "ANGEL OF PEACE," FABRIC, 16" (41 CM) HIGH. PHOTO: ANTONETTE CELY.

TRUDEL T. GIFFORD, "IN-FIN-ITY" FROM SERAPH-FIN SERIES, PAINTED TINWORK, 16" x 16" (41 x 41 CM).

DELORES DARBY SMITH, "ANGEL SERIES (ONE OF 10), POLYCHROMATIC SILKSCREEN PRINTING ON CYANOTYPE IMAGERY, 13" x 17" (33.5 x 44 CM). PHOTO: JEANETTE MILLS.

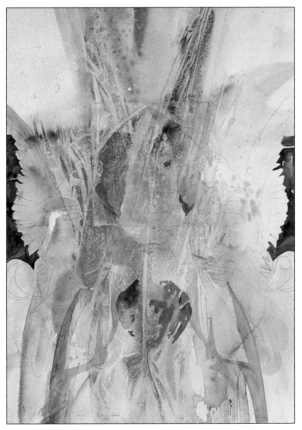

S. TUCKER COOKE, "LUCIFER'S ANGEL," CHARCOAL AND PASTEL ON PAPER, 24" x 30" (61.5 x 77 CM).

G. CAROL BOMER, "A HEART OF FLESH FOR A HEART OF STONE," WATERCOLOR ON PAPER, 22" x 30" (56.5 x 77 CM).

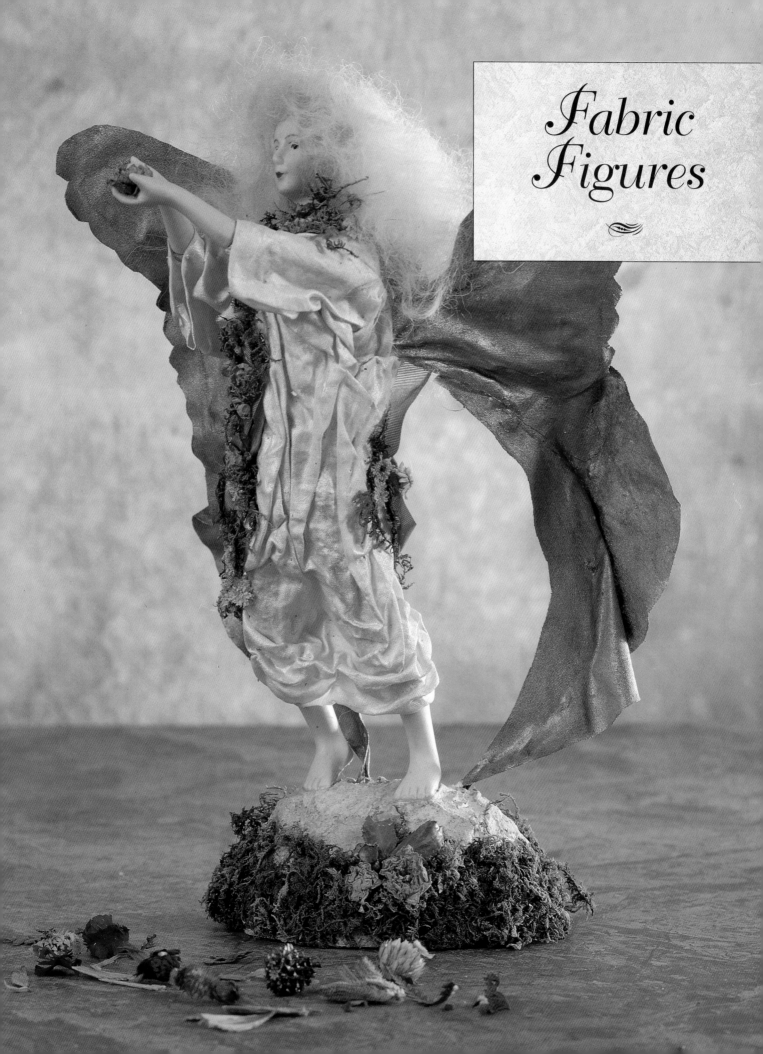

Designer:
Dolly Lutz Morris
Size:
11 inches (28 cm)

Garden Angel

To express her love of nature and gardening, designer Dolly Lutz Morris created an angel who, Dolly said, knows the flowers we enjoy are truly gifts from God. With her bare feet and windswept hair, this beautiful guardian of nature is more earthy than her heavenly counterparts.

Materials ▾

1/2 yard (46 cm) white organdy fabric

20 inches (51.5 cm) of 1/2-inch (1.5 cm) pink ribbon

porcelain 1-1/4-inch (3 cm) head*

porcelain hands and feet*

muslin doll body*

4-inch (10.5 cm) polystyrene foam egg

5 feet (154 cm) heavy-gauge wire

wool hair

paper mache mix

polyester fiberfill

dried moss, feverfew, and rosebuds

gold acrylic paint

fabric stiffener

hot glue

white glue

*head, hands, and body sold as set: Item # 161-76, Mangelsen's, 3457 S. 84th Street, Omaha, Nebraska 68127, (402) 391-6225.

Tools ▾

glue gun

wire cutters

knife

scissors

stainless steel pins

Instructions ▾

1. Make a wire armature (figure 1) to fit inside the muslin body and extremities; your angel will be stable and able to hold a pose. As shown in figure 2, the torso and leg wire is 18 inches (46 cm) long, all one piece. When you fashion the legs, bring the wire straight down from the head and make a double wire loop to create the legs. The arm wire is a separate 6-inch-long (15.5 cm) piece.

2. Sew the muslin body and insert the wire. Stuff the body with fiberfill and add the head and extremities as indicated in the manufacturer's directions.

3. Cut a piece of wire 24 inches (61.5 cm) long for the wings. Place the center of the wire at the front of the angel, just below the arms at the shoulders. Bring the wire to the back and twist it securely so it is tight around the doll.

4. Cut the polystyrene egg in half the long way to make the base. Scoop out the foam slightly in the shape of her feet and hot-glue them into the footprints.

5. Insert 1-1/2 inches (4 cm) of each end of the wing wire into the base behind her. Bend the wires to fit the curves of the wing pattern (figure 3).

6. Cover the entire egg base with a 1/3-inch (1.25 cm) layer of paper mache mix and allow it to dry thoroughly.

7. Pose the body and arms as desired.

8. Cut two 3-inch-square (8 cm) pieces of organdy. Dip them in fabric stiffener and smooth off excess. Drape them over the arms for sleeves. Pin the pieces shut at the underarm seam until dry.

9. Cut a piece of organdy 6 x 6 inches (15.5 x 15.5 cm) and dip it in stiffener, smoothing off excess. Drape it around her body to make a robe. Pin to hold in the folds until dry and pin the robe closed at the back. Let dry. Use white glue to secure the back if needed.

10. Dip the ribbon in stiffener and drape it over the shoulder at the center and down the front and back, curving it gracefully. Pin to secure until dry.

11. Cut two wing patterns from organdy (figure 3). Dip the fabric in a mixture of half stiffener and half gold acrylic paint. Smooth off excess. Place the fabric wings over the wire wings with the wire on the back side. Pin to hold the fabric to the wire and let dry. Add glue if needed to secure it to the wire. Coat the exposed wire with gold paint.

12. Glue on the wool hair.

13. Glue the moss and dried flowers to the base and the ribbon drape, using white glue. Hot-glue the rosebud to her hands.

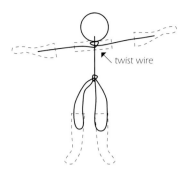

Figure 1

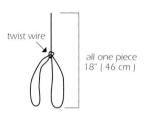

Figure 2

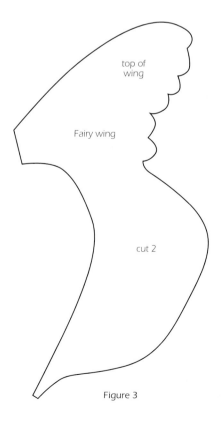

Figure 3

Enlarge 240%

Painter of Guardian Angels

Sandra Martindale, an artist living in Black Mountain, North Carolina, has seen angels all her life. About 22 years ago, while sitting in a prayer group, she saw angels hovering around people in the group and decided to draw one. Soon people started asking her to draw their angels. With today's phenomenal interest in angels, Sandi and her special gift are much in demand. She lectures, conducts workshops, and paints more and more portraits such as the one shown here. Sandi often writes about her encounters with angels, all of which she says, have a sense of "all encompassing love" about them. Here is a sampling of her thoughts on the subject, as beautifully expressed as her lovely pastel portraits.

"Is it only my imaginings or is it the opening of some secret inner ear that seems to hear soft murmurings of wings, the music of the Light? Is it only my imaginings or does some inner eye truly witness the angelic beings pouring forth some deep and total devotion, such tender love, such illuminating Light?"

Down-to-Earth Angel

According to designer Patricia Przybylinksi, this meticulously crafted purple-winged messenger is practical, easy to talk to, and spirited. Although she loves to fly, her first priority is to lend support to whoever needs her help. A divine beauty, indeed.

Designer:
Patricia Przybylinski
Size:
18 inches (46 cm)

Materials ▾

1/4 yard (23 cm) 100% cotton (unbleached muslin)

liquid dark brown dye

polyester fiberfill or fleece

1/8 yard (11.5 cm) cotton fabric of your choice for skirt

1/8 yard (11.5 cm) cotton fabric of your choice for blouse

scrap of contrasting fabric for collar

10 inches (25.5 cm) cotton ribbing material for leggings

scraps of fabric for hat

1/4 yard (23 cm) heavy weight white fabric for wings

1/4 yard (23 cm) heavy weight fusible interfacing

scraps of medium weight interfacing

5 skeins embroidery floss for face

blush or colored pencil   *(continued)*

Materials (continued) ▾

small amount 100% black lopi wool for hair

brown and black thread, and colors to match clothes

10-inch-long (25.5 cm) piece of cardboard

crafting feathers (sanitized)

buttons/jewels (optional)

hot glue

Tools ▾

glue gun

hand sewing and sewing machine equipment

pinking shears

disappearing ink pen

chopstick

Instructions ▾

1. Wash muslin, leave wet, and prepare dye according to package instructions. Dye muslin, rinse, and dry.

2. Fold the muslin in half. Using a disappearing pen, trace the upper and lower body patterns onto the material as if they are one piece (figures 1 and 2).

3. Sew the body on the traced lines, leaving an opening as indicated before cutting out the pattern. Sew the darts in the front and back of the neck (separate the layers of fabric).

4. Cut out the body, leaving about 1/8-inch (.5 cm) seam allowance; be careful not to cut too close. Also, leave a little extra seam allowance by the body side opening to make it easier to fold in and sew shut later.

5. Turn the body right side out with the aid of a chopstick. Turn one leg at a time through the body side opening, then turn each arm, and save the head for last.

6. Stuff the body carefully (and patiently!) with small, uniform bits of fiberfill. Start with the feet: stuff one foot (up to where you imagine an ankle), then stuff the other foot, stuffing both firmly. Compare the feet sizes, then continue stuffing up the leg (leaving a small break in the fiberfill to make it easier to sew up the feet in a natural position later).

7. Stuff up to each knee; sew a double line of stitching across each knee to form the knee joint. Continue stuffing each leg up to the crotch, and then sew another double line of stitches.

8. Stuff each hand, compare the sizes, then continue stuffing up to the elbows. Sew a double line of stitches for the elbow joint. Stuff up to the shoulders, compare sizes, and sew the joints, following the stitching suggestions on the pattern. Turn in the seam allowance in the side opening and sew shut.

9. Stuff the remainder of the body through the head opening, right up to within 1/4 inch (1 cm) of the top of the head. Fold in the 1/4-inch (1 cm) seam allowance, and run a gathering stitch close to the head; anchor this stitch, and oversew this seam for strength.

10. With one of your thumbs, push one angel foot up into a natural position and sew in place. Repeat with the other foot.

11. With pinking shears cut an 8 x 23-inch-wide (20.5 x 59 cm) block for the skirt. Place patterns for figures 3, 4, 5, and 6 on the fabric, and cut the number of pieces as indicated.

12. Sew the outside seam of each collar set with right sides together. Turn right side out.

13 With right sides together, sew the blouse front to the blouse back at the shoulder seams. Repeat for the lining.

14. Turn up the hem on the sleeves 1/4 inch (1 cm) and machine hem.

15. Take the pieces to the ironing board; iron open the blouse shoulder seams, iron the collar pieces flat, and iron the hemmed seam on the sleeves.

16. Lay the blouse piece (not the lining) flat with the right side up, and pin the collar pieces onto the neck edge (also right side up), starting about 1/4 inch (1 cm) from the back edge of the blouse neck. The collar pieces should meet at the center front of the blouse neck. Machine baste the collar to the neck edge.

17. With right sides together (and sandwiching collar), pin blouse lining over the blouse piece. Sew up the back edge, around neck, and down the other back edge,

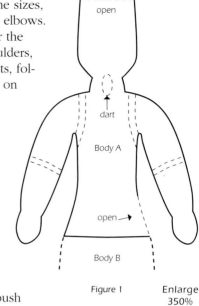

Figure 1   Enlarge 350%

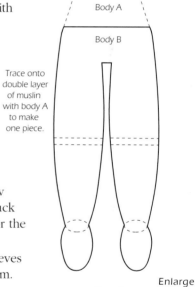

Trace onto double layer of muslin with body A to make one piece.

Figure 2   Enlarge 330%

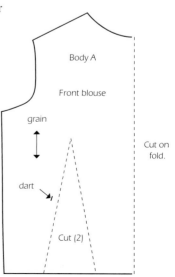

Figure 3   Enlarge 175%

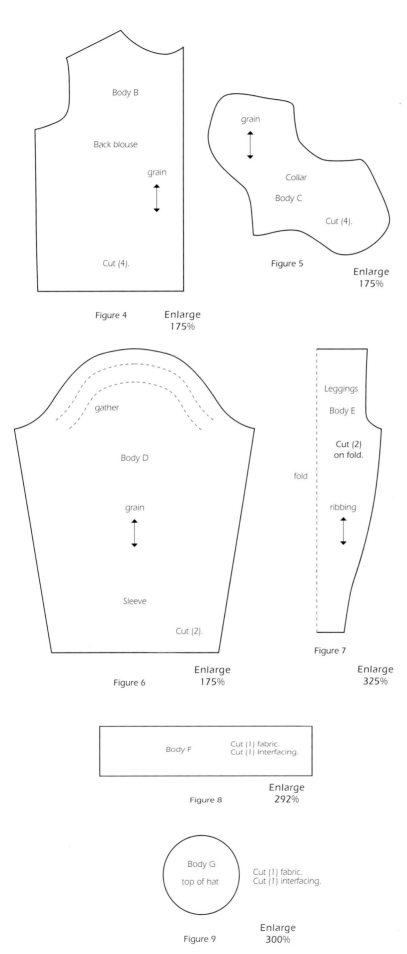

Body B

Back blouse

grain

Cut (4).

Figure 4 **Enlarge 175%**

grain

Collar

Body C

Cut (4).

Figure 5 **Enlarge 175%**

gather

Body D

grain

Sleeve

Cut (2).

Figure 6 **Enlarge 175%**

Leggings

Body E

Cut (2) on fold.

fold

ribbing

Figure 7 **Enlarge 325%**

Body F

Cut (1) fabric.
Cut (1) Interfacing.

Figure 8 **Enlarge 292%**

Body G

top of hat

Cut (1) fabric.
Cut (1) interfacing.

Figure 9 **Enlarge 300%**

leaving the sides open. (Tuck the "shoulder flap" of the collar out of the way so you don't catch it in the seam.) Check for puckers and correct if necessary. Trim and clip the neck seam. Turn right side out and iron flat.

18. Sew darts in blouse front (see figure 3) to join the lining and the blouse.

19. Sew two rows of gathering stitches on sleeve tops between dots; pull up both rows of stitches and adjust gathers. Pin the gathered sleeve to the blouse arm hole and the lining with right sides together, again adjusting the gathers. Cut off tails of gathering stitches to keep out of the way. Keep the collar free from the shoulder seam and sew the sleeve to the blouse. Sew between the rows of gathering stitches, check for puckers, and correct if needed; then remove the lower gathering stitches with a seam ripper.

20. Pin side seams together (right sides), matching sleeve bottoms and arm hole seams, and stitch right up the side and down through the sleeves. Turn right side out.

21. Machine sew the hem of the skirt. With right sides together sew center back seam (1/2-inch (1.5 cm) allowance), trim with pinking shears, and iron seam open.

22. Run two rows of gathering stitches at the top edge of skirt, first about 1/8 inch (.5 cm) from the edge, second about 1/2 inch (1.5 cm). Pull up stitches. Put the blouse inside the skirt with the blouse right side meeting skirt right side, and sew the waist seam between the rows of gathered stitches. Make sure the center back seam of skirt is centered between the side seams and blouse darts. Check for puckers, and then remove the lower row of gathered stitches. Turn dress right side out and admire your work!

23. Cut out two legging pieces (figure 7) on the fold of the cotton ribbing with the ribbing running lengthwise. Turn up a 1/4-inch (1 cm) hem and sew up the side of one leg with right sides facing; catch the turned up hem in your stitching. Repeat for other leg. Turn one leg right side out and down the inside of the other leg (this one still wrong side out), and sew crotch seam. Turn right side out.

24. To make the hat, cut figures 8 and 9 in both fabric and fusible interfacing and iron the interfacing to the fabric pieces. Cut the rosette piece (figure 10) out of contrasting fabric. Hem the bottom edge of the hat band, and sew the back seam 1/4 inch

(1 cm) with right sides facing. Pin the hat top circle to the band with right sides facing, easing the material as you pin. Sew the seam, and check to be sure you caught the layers all the way around. Iron the rosette piece in half lengthwise, and run a gathering stitch down the length opposite the fold. Pull up the stitch and gather piece into a flower shape, taking hand stitches as you roll. Hand sew it to the hat.

25. Follow the stitching suggestions in figure 11 for the face, or create your own. Use single strands of embroidery floss, stitching the face through the stuffed head, starting at the back with neat, anchored stitches. Use French knots for the eyes.

26. Wind the lopi wool around the long side of the cardboard until your neatly wound rows are about 2 inches (5 cm) wide. Cut the wool in half at one end of the cardboard and then in half again, creating a 4-inch (10.5 cm) section of 5-inch-long (13 cm) strands. Center the strands on a piece of scrap paper (figure 12) and sew a "part" using matching thread. Rip the paper away from one side of the part, then the other and you'll have created a wig for your angel.

27. Glue a "part" onto the head, starting a little off center on the forehead to the back of the head, stopping higher than the nape of the neck. Immediately place the wig's "part" onto the glue "part" and hold in place a few seconds. (Don't burn your fingers!) Let dry for 10 minutes, and then trim the hair to your liking.

28. Fold the heavy-weight fusible interfacing in half and trace one set of wings (figure 13). Cut out carefully just inside the tracing line. With an iron, fuse each wing to an appropriately sized folded square of heavy white material. Pin the folded layers of each square with the bonded wing together, and sew carefully together around the bonded wing outline, keeping open between the dots. Trim seams, turn right side out, and iron flat (folding in the seam allowance at openings). Stitch the wings together, catching the neatly ironed openings in your stitching (figure 14). Go wild with feathers, buttons, and jewels, and glue to both sides of each wing.

29. Pull the leggings up the angel's legs, and adjust the seam to run straight down the legs. Fold under the waist hem, and hand sew the legging waist to the body, gathering slightly as you sew.

30. Put the dress on, and sew shut the blouse's back opening under the collar. Trim the dress with buttons.

31. Place the wings on the back of the angel and secure with neat stitches right through the back of the dress.

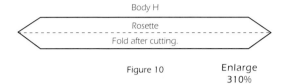

Figure 10   Enlarge 310%

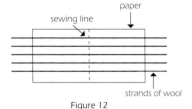

Figure 11

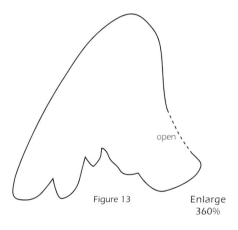

Figure 12

Figure 13   Enlarge 360%

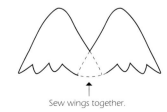

Figure 14

> ▶ *I never dreamt that tender blossoms would be brown or precious angels could come down to live in the garden of my giving heart. But here you are, brown angel.*
>
> WALTER DEAN MYERS

Winter-White Angel

As crisp and pristine as freshly fallen snow, Elsie Pugh's angel evokes all that is special about a winter day.

Designer: Elsie Pugh
Size: 12 inches (30.5 cm)

Materials ▾

12-inch (30.5 cm) white polystyrene foam cone

3-inch (1 cm) white polystyrene foam ball

1-1/2 yards (1.38 m) of 45-inch-wide (115.5 cm) white fabric

18 inches (46 cm) of 2-inch-wide (5 cm) lace

double-faced fusible webbing

3 yards (2.8 m) of narrow gold and white ribbon

36 inches (92.5 cm) of artificial pine garland

gold thread

polyester fiberfill

craft glue

Tools ▾

sewing machine equipment

floral wire

3-inch floral picks

Instructions ▾

1. Cut 1 inch (2.5 cm) off the top of the cone. Put a dab of glue on one end of a floral pick and insert it into the top of the cone. Put another dab of glue on the other end of the pick and push the foam ball onto it.

2. Cut a circle of fabric 29 inches wide (74.5 cm) and trim it with lace. Place the fabric over the angel's head and wire it around the neck.

3. To fashion the sleeves, cut a 10 x 18-inch (25.5 x 46 cm) piece of fabric; fold it lengthwise and tie a knot in the middle. Glue the knotted section to the back of the neck and bring the sleeves around front. Tuck a small amount of fiberfill into the sleeves.

4. Make a collar from the lace and glue it in place. Tie a ribbon around her neck.

5. Cut two heart-shaped pieces of fabric for wings and use the fusible webbing to join them. Trim the wings with lace and glue them on.

6. Use the fiberfill to make hair for the angel and glue it on. Make a halo with the garland and glue it on. Fashion a heart-shaped wreath and glue it to the wrists of both sleeves. Decorate the halo and heart with dried flowers.

Designer: Marj Ingalls Beaty
Size: 9 inches (15.5 cm)

A Difficult Angel

During the time designer Marj Ingalls Beaty set aside to create an angel for this book, her life was beset by a series of events that left her feeling "frayed." Much to Marj's surprise, A Difficult Angel emerged. This unique angel wants to help, but blows in late, disheveled, and unapologetic. Not surprisingly, the help she brings is laughter.

Materials ▾

1/4 yard (250 cm) muslin

1/2 yard (50 cm) cotton print or other fabric of your choice for dress

1/4 yard (25 cm) each of 3 different complementary fabrics for wings and stars

1/4 - 1 yard (25 cm - 1 m) of 4 or 5 different narrow ribbons

natural raffia for hair

3 inches (8 cm) gold or silver metallic craft cord

8 ounces (230 g) polyester fiberfill

permanent fabric marking pens in brown, blue, and red

18-inch (46 cm) length heavy-gauge floral wire

heavy-gauge thread: off-white and color that matches fabric

off-white thread

double-faced fusible interfacing

gold glitter spray

blush

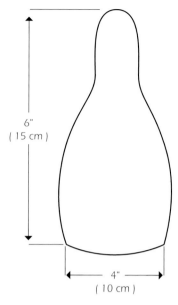

6"
(15 cm)

4"
(10 cm)

Figure 1

Figure 2

Tools ▾

hand sewing and sewing machine equipment
pinking shears

Instructions ▾

1. Draw the body shape on a double
layer of muslin (figure 1). Stitch the body,
but leave the bottom open. Cut 1/4 inch (1
cm) in from the stitching line. Clip and
turn. Stuff with fiberfill.

2. Cut a circle of fabric from the dress
material, 1/2 inch larger than the base of
the angel's body. Pin it evenly around the
base, and baste to body sides. Cover the
raw edge with ribbon or trim, and slip
stitch to secure.

3. Make the nose from a 1/2-inch (1.5
cm) circle of muslin. Gather around the
edge of the circle, stuff with a bit of fiberfill, and pull the gather closed. Stitch the
nose to the face.

4. Fold 6- to 7-inch (15 - 18 cm) lengths
of raffia in half, and stitch them at the fold
to the seam around the angel's head. Braid
or otherwise arrange the hair and stitch it
in place. Leave short ends sticking up
around the face (another bad-hair day!).

5. Draw the face with marker pens
(figure 2).

6. Fold a 15 x 16-inch (38.5 x 41 cm)
length of dress fabric as shown in figure 3.
Cut the sleeve openings 3 inches (7.5 cm)
deep on either side. Cut the neck opening
on the fold about 10 inches (26 cm) wide.
With pinking shears, trim the hem edge.

7. Cut the sleeves (figure 4). Machine
gather on the sleeve top, pin to the sleeve
opening with right sides together, and
stitch. After both sleeves are in place on the
dress, pull gathers at the bottom edge of
the sleeves to a 3-1/2-inch (9 cm) width.

Right sides together, sew a 2 x 3-1/2-inch
(5 x 9 cm) strip of muslin to each sleeve.

8. Fold the dress and sleeves right sides
together. Draw small hands on the muslin.
Machine stitch the hands, underarm seams,
and side seams of dress. Clip and turn.
Stuff the hands lightly with fiberfill. Fold
the neckline under 1/4 inch (1 cm), and
secure with hand gathering stitches.

9. For arm mobility, wrap an 18-inch (46
cm) length of heavy-gauge floral wire
around the body at shoulder level. Leave
3-1/2-inch (9 cm) sections free to form the
arms, crossing over at midback level (figures 5a and 5b). Tack the wire to the body
with heavy-gauge thread.

10. Dress the angel carefully, tucking the
wire into the sleeves and hands. Pull the
gathers closed at the neckline. Hand stitch
at the bottom of the sleeve to secure the
wire structure.

11. For wings and stars, use double-faced
fusible webbing to prevent the cut fabric
from unravelling. Fuse the fabric according
to manufacturer's directions. Cut the wings
(figure 6) from a 7 x 7-inch (18 x 18 cm)
square. The same size square will be
enough for a number of stars (figures 7 and
8). Hand stitch the wings, stars, and several
matching (or mismatching) ribbons and
bows to the dress.

12. Cut a 3- to 4-inch (8 - 10 cm) length of
gold or silver cord to fashion the halo. Tie
the circle with a square knot. Add a bow,
ribbon, or star, and sew onto the hair.

13. To make the lined tote bag, cut two rectangles each 3-1/2 x 6 inches (9 x 15.5 cm),
out of complementary fabrics. Right sides
together, sew a 1/4-inch (1 cm) seam along
the 6-inch (15.5 cm) edge. Open it out and
fold lengthwise. Right sides together,
machine stitch the edges, leaving the narrow
bottom edge of lining open for turning.

14. Align the seams on the bottom corners
of the bag. Machine stitch across the seam.
Clip the triangular edge away from stitching, and turn. Fold the open end under
1/4 inch (1 cm), and slip stitch closed.

15. Make a handle for the bag out of ribbon, cord, or fabric, affixed with a hand-
stitched star. Fill the bag with extra stars, and
hand stitch it to the angel's hand or sleeve.

16. To finish, apply blush to the face and
nose, and spray generously all over with
gold glitter.

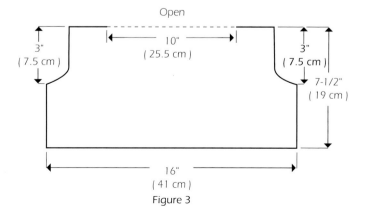

Open

3"
(7.5 cm)

10"
(25.5 cm)

3"
(7.5 cm)

7-1/2"
(19 cm)

16"
(41 cm)

Figure 3

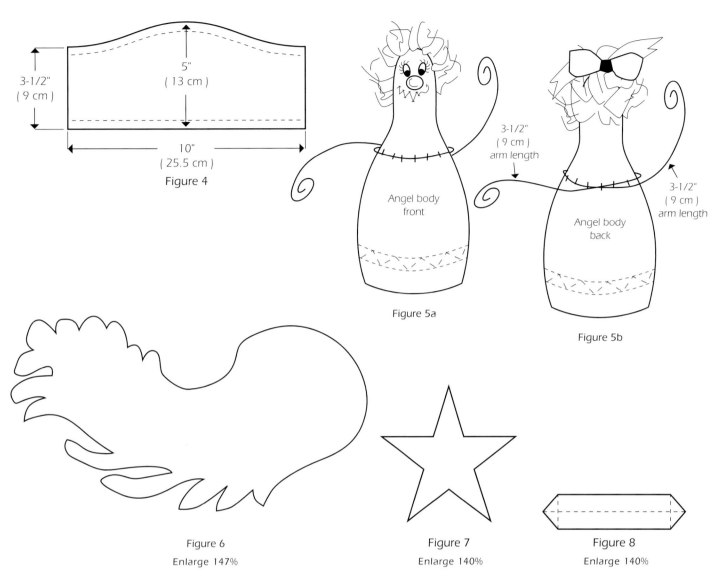

3-1/2"
(9 cm)

5"
(13 cm)

10"
(25.5 cm)

Figure 4

Angel body
front

Figure 5a

3-1/2"
(9 cm)
arm length

3-1/2"
(9 cm)
arm length

Angel body
back

Figure 5b

Figure 6

Enlarge 147%

Figure 7

Enlarge 140%

Figure 8

Enlarge 140%

Handkerchief Angels

To preserve a bit of history, designer Pam Forsythe suggests making these lovely angels out of handkerchiefs or napkins that are either antiques or family heirlooms.

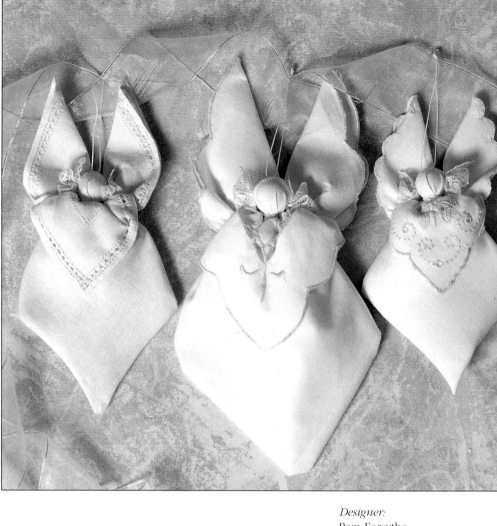

Materials ▾

square handkerchief or napkin (linen is the best)

iron-on heavy-weight interfacing or craft bond

3/4 inch - 1 inch (2 x 1.5 cm) round wooden bead

small scrap of white or off-white fabric

10 inches (25.5 cm) lace to match

white thread

8 inches (20.5 cm) white string or narrow ribbon

spray starch

Tools ▾

hand sewing equipment

Instructions ▾

1. Spray the handkerchief with spray starch and iron it.

2. Choose the prettiest corner of your handkerchief to become the front of your finished angel.

3. Cut two 4-inch-square (10.5 cm) pieces of interfacing. Fuse them to the right side of the two corners adjacent to the "pretty" side. These corners are the wing corners (figure 1).

4. Fold the handkerchief in half diagonally, with the right side of the pretty corner to the inside (figure 2).

5. Fold the pretty corner down towards the center fold and the "back" corner toward the back of the work (figures 3 and 4).

6. To make the angel's head, cover a wooden bead with a small scrap of fabric and secure it with a needle and thread (figure 5).

7. Place the head so it shows above the pretty corner and the ragged edge of the

fabric scrap lies between—hidden by the folded edge (figure 6). Secure with hand stitches.

8. Center the lace on top of the head and secure it with hand stitches, making two loops of lace on each side at ear level (figure 7).

9. Unfold the back corner so it lies behind the angel's head. Run a loose gathering thread along the folds beside the head going through all thicknesses (figure 8). Start at the outer edge and go toward the head, ending with a needle and thread at the back. Pull both sides tight and secure with a few stitches behind the head.

10. Run a loose gathering thread from a point about halfway between the head and the wing corner, straight across to the bottom of the work. Pull tight and secure with a knot (figure 9).

11. Fold the wings to the back of the work and secure with stitches, folding excess fabric between the body and wings (figure 10).

12. Turn the angel over, spread the wings, and fold the back corner down between

Designer:
Pam Forsythe

Size: 8 - 16 inches (20.5 - 41 cm) square

them. Secure at the sides with a few stitches connecting the back corner to the body of the angel.

13. Attach a short length of string or ribbon to the head for a hanger.

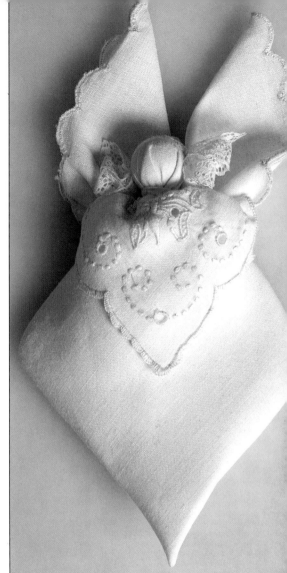

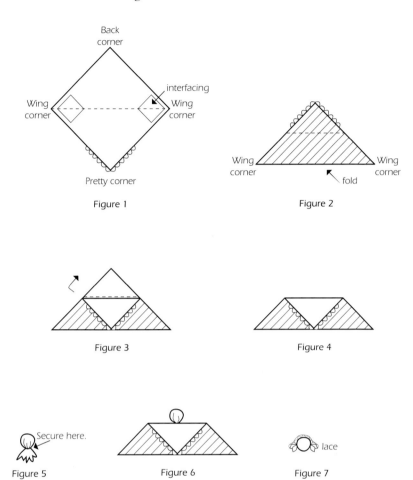

Figure 1

Figure 2

Figure 3

Figure 4

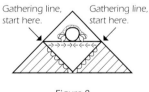

Figure 5

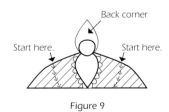

Figure 6

Figure 7

Figure 8

Figure 9

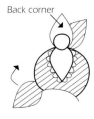

Figure 10

Key :

☐ Right side of fabric

▨ Wrong side of fabric

- - - - Fold line

⇢⇢⇢⇢ Gathering line with direction of fabric

Designers: Nan and Bill Parker
Size: 12 inches (30.5 cm)

> **► Be not forgetful
> to entertain
> strangers, for
> thereby some
> have entertained
> angels unawares.**
>
> HEBREWS 13:2

Dinner Napkin Angel

*This simple and clever design by Nan and Bill Parker
transforms a serviette into a celestial server.*

Materials ▾

1/3 yard (31 cm) tea-dyed muslin

6 x 6 inches (15 x 15 cm) brown cotton
    fabric

5 x 12 inches (13 x 30.5 cm) gold lamé
    fabric

scraps of fabric with angel motifs

12 x 24 inches (30.5 x 62 cm) slip fabric

large dinner napkin

12 inches (30.5 cm) narrow ribbon

metallic gold craft cord with stars

thick polyester fleece lining

polyester fiberfill

gold fabric paint

black yarn

permanent fabric marking pens: black,
    white, and red

blush for cheeks

small strand of craft pearls

miniature artificial roses and baby's breath

hot glue

6-inch (15 cm) wooden stand (optional)

Tools ▾

hand sewing and sewing machine
  equipment

glue gun

Instructions ▾

1. Using muslin, make the doll body and arms using a basic pattern of your choice. Make the head with the brown fabric.

2. Stuff the head, body, and arms lightly with fiberfill. Attach the arms to the body. If you are planning to make a stand, leave a small opening in the bottom of the torso where the stand will be inserted. Without a stand, the angel makes a lovely tree-topper.

3. Make the slip and glue it to the torso.

4. Fold the napkin lengthwise. Find the center and cut a very small hole. Insert the head through the opening. Turn under the edge of the napkin around the neck opening. Gather stitch and knot tightly.

5. Gather the napkin over each shoulder. Bring the arms to the front. Lay the angel down; bring both edges of the front half of the napkin to the back of the body and secure with hot glue. (This gives the effect of having a robe over the dress.)

6. Tack the hands in place. Glue on the dried flowers and the ribbon bow.

7. Wind the black yarn around two fingers to create the hair and tie in the center. Glue to the head. Fashion a halo from the gold cord and glue on. Glue on the necklace.

8. Draw on the face.

9. Make a pattern for the wings, cut out the fabric and the fleece, and sew together. Glue on the wings.

10. Attach the doll to the stand.

► *Their faces were living flame; their wings were gold; and for the rest their white was so intense, no snow can match the white they showed. When they climbed down into that flowering Rose, from rank to rank, they shared that peace and ardor which they gained, with wings that fanned their sides.*

DANTE

PARADISO, XXXI

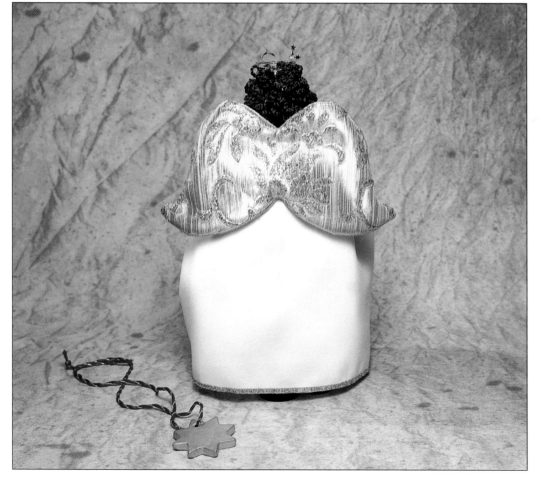

Pheasant Angel

With feathers given to her by an avid hunter friend, designer Dolly Lutz Morris captures the spirit of the wild in this beautiful angel.

► *The garments of the angels correspond to their intelligence. The garments of some glitter as with flame, and those of others are resplendent as with light: others are of various colors, and some white and opaque.*

EMANUEL SWEDENBORG

Designer: Dolly Lutz Morris

Size: 12 inches (31 cm)

Materials ▾

pheasant feathers

2 pheasant wings*

9-inch (23 cm) polystyrene foam cone

1/3 yard (31 cm) gold lamé fabric

18 inches (46 cm) of 1-3/8-inch (1.25 cm)
    gold ribbon

matching thread

1-1/2-inch (4 cm) wooden ball for head

self-hardening clay for hands

fabric stiffener

13 inches (33.5 cm) heavy-gauge wire

acrylic paints: flesh, brown, black, and red

plastic wrap

hot glue

*Or use individual feathers glued to a stiffened
    muslin backing*

Tools ▾

hand sewing and sewing machine
    equipment

glue gun

wire cutters

Instructions ▾

1. Glue the wooden ball to the top of
the cone.

2. Bend the wire around the top of cone
at the center and extend it down both
sides to make the 5-inch-long (13 cm)
arms.

3. Use the clay to form simple scoop-
shaped hands over the ends of the wire.
Let dry.

4. With the acrylic paints, paint the clay
hands flesh color.

5. Paint the hair and face on the wooden
ball.

6. Fold the fabric in half (figure 1); then
fold it in half the other way (figure 2). You
will have a fold at the top and a fold on
the right edge. Place the pattern (figure 3)
on the fabric with the top sleeve edge and
the center of the robe on the folds. Cut
out. Stitch up the outside skirt and arm
seams.

7. For this step, protect the angel's face
by covering it with a piece of plastic wrap.
Turn the robe right side out and dip it into
fabric stiffener, smoothing off excess. With
needle and thread, turn the neck edge
under 1/4 inch (1 cm) and run a gather
stitch around it. Don't pull tight. Place the

robe on the angel, pull up the gathers at
the neck, and knot.

8. Turn the sleeve edges under 1/4 inch
(1 cm) and run a gather stitch around
them. Pull the gathers tight at the wrist,
and knot.

9. Run a gather stitch around the bottom
of the skirt that has been turned under 1/4
inch (1 cm). Pull tight and knot with the
gathers at the base of the cone. Work the
drapes of the skirt to achieve a pleasing
look. Set the doll on plastic wrap and
allow the fabric stiffener to dry. Remove
the plastic wrap from her face.

10. With hot glue, affix feathers to the
front of the robe, taking care not to get
glue on the front of the feathers. Glue the
two pheasant wings to her back.

11. Adorn the angel with gold ribbon.
Glue ribbon to her back to hide where
you attached the wings.

▶ *So many wings*

come here

dipping honey

and speak here

in your home

Oh God.

AZTEC POEM

Figure 1   Figure 2

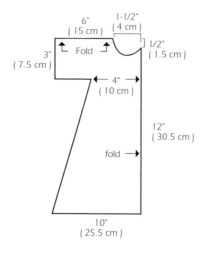

Figure 3

Naimy

Nan and Bill Parker named this charming angel for all the special Nancys and the one special Amy in their family.

Materials ▾

1/3 yard (31 cm) tea-dyed muslin

1-1/2 yards (138.5 cm) curtain fabric for dress and pantaloons

1/3 yard (31 cm) fabric of your choice for wings and heart

scrap of fabric for bib (piece of linen handkerchief)

polyester fleece lining

polyester fiberfill

embroidery thread

yarn for hair

pearl cotton

permanent fabric marking pens in black and red

blush for cheeks and eyes

miniature basket

dried flowers, small pinecones, and Spanish moss

metallic gold craft cord with stars

metal stand

hot glue

> ► *So in a voice,*
> *so in a*
> *shapeless flame*
> *Angels affect us*
> *oft, and*
> *worshipped be.*
>
> JOHN DONNE

Tools ▾

hand sewing and sewing machine equipment

large hand sewing needle

glue gun

Designers: Nan and Bill Parker
Size: 15 inches (38 cm)

Instructions ▾

1. Using muslin, make the doll using a basic pattern of your choice. Stuff the parts lightly with fiberfill.

2. Cut out the dress, heart-shaped wings, and pantaloons. Serge or zigzag the seams.

3. Appliqué the hearts on the dress and bib.

4. Assemble the dress and pantaloons.

5. Gather the arms, waist, and cuffs with pearl cotton using a large needle. Tie the bows.

6. Dress the doll.

7. Glue on the hair. Glue the head to the body, adding metallic gold cord as a halo.

8. Cut out the fabric and the fleece lining for the 8-inch-wide (20.5 cm) heart and sew together. Glue on the wings.

9. Glue Spanish moss, pinecones, and flowers into the basket.

10. Glue the hands together with the basket between them.

11. Draw on the face.

12. Position the doll on the stand.

Flying Angels

These extraordinary, life-size heavenly hosts were created as Christmas decorations for a church sanctuary. Designers Diane Kroll and Beverly Gottfried recommend working with a friend on this ambitious project.

Designers: Diane Kroll and Beverly Gottfried
Size: 6 feet (185 cm)

Materials ▾

For each angel:

lightweight polystyrene foam wig head

1 bag curly doll hair

1 pair latex surgical gloves

1 pair flesh-colored socks

fake eyelashes

1 gold star garland for halo

1 wire tomato cage

chicken wire, two pieces: 10 inches x 4
  feet (25.5 x 123 cm); 4 x 7 feet (123 cm
  x 2.1 m)

75-100 plastic grocery bags

3 yards (3 m) gold roping for belt

4 wire coat hangers

8 yards (8 m) white muslin

1 gallon white glue

straight pins

hot glue

sewing thread

latex or acrylic paint: flesh, pink, red, and
  brown

gold glitter

purchased trumpet

enamel spray paint: white, teal, and gold

plastic sheeting

masking tape

heavy-gauge wire

sponge

polyester fiberfill

For angel with banner:

4 satin Christmas tree ornament balls

2 empty paper towel rolls

1 x 3 feet (30.5 x 92.5 cm) good quality paper

black marker

Tools ▾

glue gun

hand or machine sewing equipment

paintbrushes

wire cutters

Making the Form

Head

1. Paint the entire wig form with flesh-colored paint.

2. Paint on the eyebrows and lashes (eye should look closed). Paint the lips and add blush color to the cheeks.

3. Separate and comb the doll hair; attach it to the head with white glue. You may need to paint the wig form dark brown if you're using brown hair.

4. Carve out the bottom of the wig form so that the wires of the tomato cage will fit inside.

Bodice

1. Press and tape the prongs of the tomato cage together in tepee fashion.

2. Push the wig form onto the prongs of the cage until the head is secure. Make sure that one spine of the cage forms a backbone. This will make suspension of the angel much easier.

3. Using the photograph as your guide, tilt the head of the hanging angel upward slightly to look as if she's blowing a trumpet. Tilt the vertical angel's head slightly upward. Tape or glue the head securely into place.

Wire Skirt

1. Cut a piece of chicken wire 7 feet (2.1 m) wide and 4 feet (123 cm) tall. Gather the wire into soft vertical folds and attach to the bottom of the tomato cage by twisting the wires together to form a seam.

2. Hold the flying angel form in a horizontal position and shape the wire skirt as desired. Create hips, and make a space in the back of the skirt where the feet will protrude. Work the standing angel in the vertical position.

Wings

1. Take the wire coat hangers apart and join two to make a circle.

2. Shape each circle to resemble one wing.

Dressing the Form

Soak all the fabric in a solution made with one part water to three parts white glue.

Skirt

1. Soak 3 yards (3 m) of the muslin in the glue medium. When the fabric is thoroughly wet, remove it from the solution and wring out the excess glue. Straighten out the fabric before draping it on the form.

2. Suspend the flying angel from the ceiling at a good working height; stand the vertical angel on the floor. Place the fabric on the skirt form and use straight pins to secure the skirt. The main seam should be along the back of the skirt. For the vertical angel, drape the fabric so that about 5 inches falls in soft ruffles on the floor. Allow to dry overnight.

Bodice

1. Form the bodice shape by taping wadded plastic bags all over the torso.

2. Soak 2 yards (2 m) of fabric in the glue and wring out slightly. Drape the fabric around the bodice and create a ruffle at the neck—the base of the wig form. Gather the ruffle up around the neck with thread and shape it into a nice collar.

3. Continue to cover the bodice with the fabric, shaping and pinning into place as you go along. Allow the piece to dry overnight.

Arms

1. Roll the 10-inch x 4-feet (26 x 123 cm) piece of chicken wire into a long tube. Attach the tube to the back of the torso, bending the loose wires onto the tomato cage to secure.

2. Bend the arms around the torso to the front of the chest and shape the arms as needed so the angel can hold a trumpet, or shape the arms to the front for the angel holding the banner.

3. Using plastic bags and tape, shape the shoulders and arms.

4. Dip 2 yards (2 m) of the fabric into the glue, squeeze out the excess, and drape the fabric over the wire shoulders and arms. The main seam should be under the arms. Try to achieve a sleeve effect.

Wings

1. Cover the wire wing forms loosely with dry fabric and hand or machine sew the fabric into place over the form.

2. Place the wings on the plastic sheeting. Sponge the glue mixture onto the wings, back and front, and allow to dry overnight.

3. When the wings are dry, peel the plastic away. The patches of glue that are visible will look great after they're painted gold.

Banner (for vertical angel)

1. Glue two satin Christmas balls at either end of two empty paper towel rolls. Spray this base with gold paint.

2. Make a paper banner that reads "Peace on Earth" or "Joy to the World" and glue it onto the base.

3. Wire the banner to the angel's arms. You do not need to make hands for this angel.

Finishing

1. Cover the angel's head with a plastic bag and spray the entire angel with white enamel paint. While the paint is wet, you may add glitter if you like.

2. Stuff the latex gloves and the socks with fiberfill and shape into hands and feet.

3. Attach the hands and feet to the angel with hot glue and tape.

4. Glue on the trumpet.

5. Spray the wings with gold paint. When the gold is dry, accent the wings with the teal spray paint.

6. For a halo, glue on the gold star garland.

7. Cut several wire strips, each about 6 inches (15.5 cm) long. Attach the wings to the angel's back using wire and hot glue.

▶ *Angels can fly because they take themselves lightly.*

Scottish Saying

Paper Mache

Designer: Dolly Lutz Morris
Size: 7 x 10 inches (18 x 25.5 cm)

Moon and Stars Angel

Make a wish on the falling star this magical angel has caught, and your wish will come true, promises designer Dolly Lutz Morris.

Materials ▾

carbon paper

paper mache mix

1/4-inch (1 cm) dowel or pencil

heavy cardboard or posterboard

acrylic paints in colors of your choice

packing tape

floral foam

spray sealer, matte finish

white glue

plastic wrap

Tools ▾

metal nail file or sculpting tools

scissors

saw

mixing bowl

paintbrushes

sharp knife

hair dryer (optional)

Instructions ▾

1. Trace and cut the pattern (including the wings) from heavy cardboard.

2. With a knife, carve the base, approximately 1-1/2 x 2-1/2 x 4 inches (4 x 6.5 x 10 cm), from the floral foam.

3. With a small saw, cut the dowel or pencil to a 5-inch length.

4. Coat 1-1/2 inches (4 cm) of the dowel or pencil tip with glue and place into the top of the base; allow to dry thoroughly.

5. Cover the base with a layer of the paper mache and blend it onto the dowel to make the stand more secure. Dry two to three days, depending on humidity and weather.

6. Secure the moon/angel figure onto the dowel with the packing tape, going over the area several times to ensure a tight fit.

7. Working on the moon portion only, cover one side with a 1/4-inch (1 cm) layer of the paper mache. Place the covered side

on your worktable which has been covered with plastic wrap. Paper mache the other side, blending all the edges and smoothing well. Stand the figure upright and allow it to dry completely.

8. When the moon area is dry, begin to flesh out the angel by building up thin layers of paper mache, smoothing, blending, and adding details as you go. Use the metal file or a sculpting tool to create the effect you like. There is no right or wrong way to sculpt. Work patiently, using thin layers, and be as imaginative as you wish.

9. Using the pattern provided, cut angel wings from heavy cardboard or posterboard and glue them onto the angel's back and the sides of the moon.

10. The angel's hair, arms, hands, feet, star, and gown folds are fashioned in the same manner, by building up thin layers of the paper mache and sculpting them into shape with your nail file or sculpting tool. This step will take time, so you may want to use a hair dryer to speed the drying time between layers.

11. Allow the angel to dry very thoroughly, and then paint it with acrylics and allow it to dry.

12. Spray the figure with two or three coats of matte sealer, allowing drying time between coats.

13. With the gold acrylic paint and a dry brush, highlight the angel's hair.

14. Paint the gold stars or moons on the base.

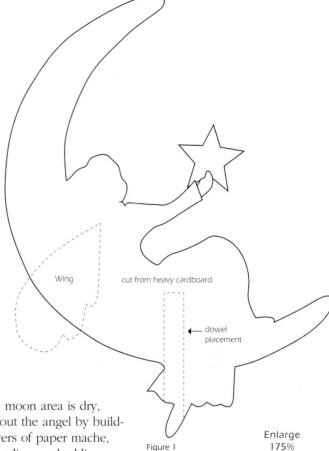

Wing

cut from heavy cardboard

← dowel placement

Figure 1

Enlarge 175%

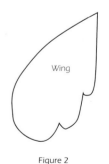

Wing

Figure 2

Enlarge 200%

Batik Angel Box

Believed to have originated on the island of Java, batik *is an ancient art usually executed on fabric. To create these stunning boxes, designer George Summers, Jr. used batik over paper mache, and the result is exquisite.*

Designer: George Summers, Jr.
Size: 7 inches (18 cm)

Materials ▾

boxes of heavy card (hat boxes and cigar
    boxes are good)

beeswax

smooth newsprint or brown kraft paper

flour and water for paste

liquid dyes

spray varnish

Tools ▾

electric deep fryer or double boiler

assorted bristle brushes

watercolor brushes

drawing pencil

Instructions ▾

1. Mix the flour and water to form a
smooth paste. Add water until the lumps
are gone the paste is slightly thicker than
white glue.

2. Cut or tear the paper into even strips.
Apply the paper strips to the box, pasting
with the flour-water medium. Cover the
entire box, inside and out, and try to
smooth out any wrinkles or air bubbles
that appear on the surface. Allow the box
to dry completely at this point, and wipe
any dusty residue off the dry box with a
damp paper towel.

3. Draw your design onto the box with a
light pencil. You can freehand your own
design or trace one from a book or card.

4. Melt the wax in a double boiler or
deep fryer. Wax should be melted enough
to apply easily with a brush.

5. With a small brush, trace your pencil
outline with the wax. These are your *resist
lines*; they will keep the dye from spilling
across the borders of your design.

6. Using watercolor brushes, paint on the
liquid dye. Allow the piece to dry completely before proceeding.

7. Spray the box with varnish. Apply several coats, allowing drying time between each
one. Do not apply varnish with a brush,
because this will disturb the wax and dye.

▶ *I looked up at the clouds, and two men were coming there, headfirst like arrows*

slanting down; and as they came they sang a sacred song and the thunder was

like drumming. I will sing it for you. The song and the drumming were like this:

"Behold a sacred voice is calling you;

All over the sky a sacred voice is calling."

BLACK ELK SPEAKS

Angel Quartet

Designed by Virginia Boegli, these joyful angels, gracious and elegant in appearance, are actually crafted from paper towels and ingenuity.

Designer: Virginia Boegli
Size: 8 x 10 inches (20.5 x 25.5 cm)

Materials ▾

1 roll of thick white paper towels

4 cups (1 liter) of prepared cellulose wallpaper paste

1-1/2 cups (360 ml) of white glue

acrylic paints (see steps 24-25)

1 roll of aluminum foil

6-inch (15.5 cm) piece of fine filament synthetic rope (for hair, method 1)

12-inch (31 cm) piece of rayon cording (for hair, method 2)

6-inch (15.5 cm) costume jewelry chain (for halo, optional)

small piece of thin wire or twist tie

large aluminum foil pie plate

thick plastic sheeting

large cookie sheet

small pear-shaped balloon (water balloon size)

Tools ▾

2-inch (5 cm) paint or pastry brush

size 10 to 12 round acrylic artist's brush

size 3 to 5 round acrylic artist's brush

small pliers with a wire cutter

toothpicks

Instructions ▾

1. Fold a 6 x 15-inch (15.5 x 38.5 cm) strip of aluminum foil into a ring-shaped collar.

2. Inflate the balloon and place it, large end down, into the collar. Adjust the collar so that it will hold the balloon upright. Set the collar and balloon on the inverted pie plate (figure 1).

3. Make your paste by combining four cups (1 liter) of the wallpaper paste with 1-1/2 cups (360 ml) of the white glue.

4. Make your paper mache medium: with the 2-inch (5 cm) brush, spread a layer of the paste onto the cookie sheet, covering an area slightly larger than one paper towel. Place one towel on top of the paste. Apply another layer of paste over the towel. Add another towel and another layer of paste. This is your mache.

5. Drape the mache over the balloon and collar to make a cone which will be the base for your angel's robe (figure 2). Set the cone aside to dry.

6. Make another batch of mache, but this time make it on your plastic sheeting. With your fingers, gently pull apart the towels, tearing them down the center. Shape the pieces into wings, and shape a tab, perpendicular to the wing, which will be used to attach the wing to the angel (figure 3). Set the wings aside to dry, about one day.

7. To make the angel's head, torso, and arms, make two foil strips, one 6 x 12 inches (15.5 x 31 cm) and one 6 x 15 inches (15.5 x 38.5 cm).

8. To make head and torso, fold the shorter strip in thirds, lengthwise. Make your folds loose and soft (figure 4a). Now make a soft fold in the middle of the strip, creating an upside-down "U" (figure 4b). Shape the head by gathering the two sides of the "U" together about 3 inches (7.5 cm) up from the bottom. Shape a narrow neck and an oval head (figure 4c).

9. To make the arms, fold the longer foil strip lengthwise in the same manner as the shorter one. Place the head and torso figure on the middle of the arm strip (figure 5a) and wrap the arm strips around the torso, crossing over the chest and bending the strips down to form the shoulders (figure 5b). Shape the arms and hands.

10. Make more mache on your cookie sheet. Tear the mache into strips and cover the head, arms and most of the torso with the medium. Wrap the mache firmly as you go, being careful not to make the figure too bulky. Also, press the mache into place; this will squeeze out any excess water. Leave 1-inch (2.5 cm) aluminum foil "tails" at the bottom of the torso.

11. Place the torso onto the cone, and press the aluminum foil "tails" gently into the angel's robe (figure 6a).

12. With two long, narrow strips of mache, anchor the torso to the robe by criss-crossing the strips over the shoulders (figure 6b). Make certain the foil is covered. Set the figure aside to dry.

13. While the wings are still attached to the plastic sheeting, paint them with the paste and set them aside to dry.

14. When the angel figure is thoroughly dry, make more mache on the cookie sheet and continue to cover the head, hands, and torso until you have achieved the look you want. Also, fashion the sleeves at this time (figure 7).

15. Make more mache as needed to fashion the angel's draped robe; turn under the raw edges on the sides and bottom for a smooth finish. Tie a rayon cord around the angel's waist, if you like, and coat the cord with paste to hold it in place (figure 8).

16. Peel the wings from the plastic sheeting. Apply paste to the newly-exposed surfaces, and set the wings aside to dry.

17. When the wings are dry, apply paste liberally to the tab portions. Wait a few minutes for the paste to penetrate the tabs; they should be pliable and sticky. Meanwhile, apply white glue to that area of the angel's back where the wings will be attached.

18. Make two loosely-crumbled balls of aluminum foil, about the size of large oranges and set them aside.

19. Position the wings on the angel's back. Press firmly and hold for a few minutes until set (figures 9a and 9b).

20. Gently lay the angel down on a hard surface. Place the foil balls under the wings to support them while they dry. Make sure the wings are in the position you want and that they are well-supported. Allow the wings to dry thoroughly.

21. To make the angel's hair, use either method below.

Method one: Untwist the piece of rope, which is twice as long as you want the angel's hair to be (figure 10a). Twist the wire

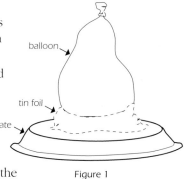

balloon

tin foil

plate

Figure 1

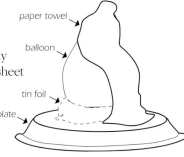

paper towel

balloon

tin foil

plate

Figure 2

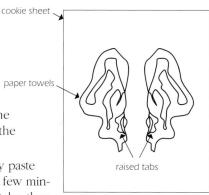

cookie sheet

paper towels

raised tabs

Figure 3

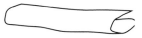

Figure 4a

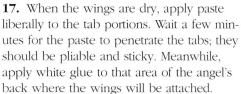

Figure 4b

Figure 4c

Figure 5a

Figure 5b

Figure 6a

Figure 6b

Figure 7

Figure 8

press here

Side

Figure 9a

Back

Figure 9b

around the rope at mid point to keep the fibers from tangling (figure 10b). Holding the hair by its wire, swish the fibers in warm water until they are relaxed. Press out the excess water. Lay the hair on the cookie sheet and coat the hair well with paste. Paste both sides. Place the hair on the angel's head and style as you like (10c).

Method two: Make the hair strands from thin mache strips. Place the strips on the angel's head and style as desired.

22. Set the angel aside to dry thoroughly.

23. Using the large artist's brush, coat the angel (except wings) all over with paste, being careful to get the paste into all the folds. Allow to dry.

24. Using the small artist's brush and acrylic paints, make a wash with a tiny dab of paints until you have the desired flesh tone. For caucasian color, use red and yellow only. For a black angel, add a touch of burnt umber to the red and yellow. For an Asian skin tone, cut back on the red and add more yellow. Test your colors on a white paper towel before painting your angel. And remember, these colors should be translucent "washes", not opaque colors.

25. When painting the angel's hair, also use red, yellow and burnt umber. Yellow with a touch of burnt umber makes blonde. Add red paint to create an auburn effect. Adding more burnt umber should give you brunette tones.

26. Using the tip of a nearly-dry artist's brush, take up a tiny dab of burnt umber and paint a single horizontal stroke for each angel eye.

27. If you wish to give your angel a halo, cut your costume jewelry chain into the desired size using your wire cutters. Use your toothpick to apply several dots of white glue to the angel's head; then put the chain in place and allow it to dry.

28. Finally, pry your finished angel off the pie plate. She should pop right off, but you may need to pry her up with a butter knife in spots. Remove the balloon and the foil collar. Your angel is finished!

Note: When directions say "allow to dry thoroughly," usually drying time is 24 hours. You may wish to complete as many steps as possible at once so several steps can be drying at the same time.

Figure 10a

Figure 10b

Figure 10c

Red-Headed Angel Ornament

If you like the dimensional effect of wood ornaments, but don't have a jigsaw, try this flame-haired celestial developed by Dolly Lutz Morris.

Materials ▾

carbon paper

cardboard

paper mache mix

acrylic paints: white, blue, and red

antiquing medium*

red wool doll hair

spray sealer

heavy-weight gold thread

paper clip

white glue

brown stain mixed with paint thinner or brown acrylic thinned with water makes an excellent medium

Tools ▾

scissors

metal nail file

large sewing needle

toothpick

paintbrushes

soft cloth scrap

Instructions ▾

1. Using carbon paper, trace the pattern onto the cardboard and cut out.

2. Cover the cut-outs with a 1/4-inch (1 cm) layer of paper mache, mixed per manufacturer's instructions. Shape and smooth all the edges with the nail file.

3. While the paper mache is wet, insert the paper clip into the back of the head, leaving a small bit exposed at the top.

4. Using the toothpick, poke holes into the hands, shoulders, tops of arms, tops of legs, bottom of skirt, and center of heart. Make sure the holes go all the way through the piece.

5. Let pieces dry and then paint.

6. Spray them with sealer and let dry.

7. Brush each piece with antiquing medium and wipe with a soft cloth until you achieve the desired aged effect; let dry.

8. Spray the pieces with sealer and let dry.

Designer: Dolly Lutz Morris
Size: 4 x 7 inches (10 x 18 cm)

9. Glue on the wings.

10. With gold thread, sew the pieces together and tie knots in each thread. Place a dot of white glue on each knot to keep the thread from ravelling.

11. Glue on red wool for hair. Attach a 4-inch (10.5 cm) length of gold thread to the paper clip for a hanger.

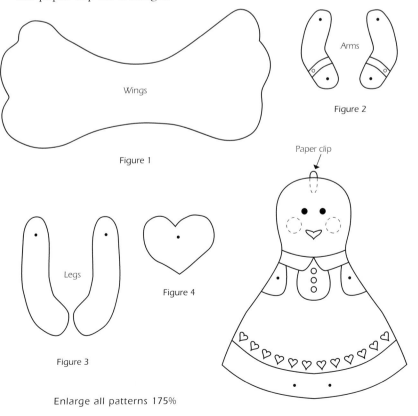

Wings

Figure 1

Arms

Figure 2

Legs

Figure 3

Figure 4

Paper clip

Figure 5

Enlarge all patterns 175%

Angelena Praying and Genevieve with Flowers

The paper mache faces on these angels give them their distinctive personalities. Designer Christi Hensley dips the painted heads in hot wax to give her musical messengers a heavenly glow.

Designer: Christi Hensley
Size: 20 inches (51.5 cm)

Materials ▾

3/4 yard (69.5 cm) fabric, either white eyelet or print for dress

1/4 yard (23 cm) muslin for wings

polyester fiberfill

rubber bands

posterboard

12 inches (31 cm) aluminum foil

paper mâché mix

2 pounds (920 g) candle wax

doll hair - curly synthetic

6 inches (15.5 cm) paper twist for halo

8 inches (20.5 cm) ribbon or gold cord

gesso sealer

acrylic paints: light flesh, light brown, blue, black, white, red, and pink

hot glue

empty coffee can

scrap of soft cloth

Variations for Genevieve

gold puffed wings (premade at crafts stores)

gold wrapping paper

gold fabric paint

small basket

dried flowers

Tools ▾

paintbrushes

sandpaper

glue gun

sewing machine (optional)

Instructions ▾

1. Using the aluminum foil, form a ball (the size and shape of a small egg), leaving a neck stem about 1/2-inch (1.5 cm) wide and 1-1/2-inches (4 cm) long (figure 1).

2. Prepare the paper mache mix according to package directions. Mold the paper mache over the foil head, about 1/4-inch (1 cm) thick. Do not form the features yet. Let dry.

3. Mold the nose, cheeks, and chin. This can take a few layers; let it dry between each application.

4. With sandpaper, smooth up the head and face.

5. Apply two coats of gesso. Paint the head flesh color and let dry. Pencil on the eyes and mouth. Paint the entire eye area white. Then paint the irises blue, the pupils black, and the lips red. Outline the eyes with black and add lashes; add white high-

lights to the irises. Paint the eyebrows light brown. Use a thin coat of pink for the cheeks, applied to the face with a dry brush.

6. Place the wax in the coffee can and put the can into a pan of water. Heat slowly to a temperature of 190 degrees Fahrenheit. Holding the head by the end of the neck, dip it into the wax completely. Remove the head in one continuous movement, tilting the features up so the excess wax drips to the back of the head. Let it dry for a few minutes and dip again; repeat the process three times. The wax may cloud over but it will clear when cool. Buff the head with a soft cloth. Note: you may want to practice the dipping process on an apple on a stick.

7. Glue will not stick to wax, so the head must be scraped from the hairline back. Use hot glue to attach the hair, following directions on the package.

8. Shape the halo from the paper twist

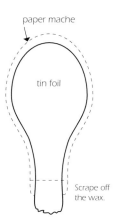

paper mache

tin foil

Scrape off the wax.

Figure 1

Figure 2

and decorate it with ribbons. Glue it to the head.

9. Fashion the hands from paper mache. For Genevieve, form two hands (figure 2), let dry, and paint. For Angelena's praying hands: Take a 5 x 5-inch (13 x 13 cm) piece of aluminum foil and fold to 1/2 x 5 inches (1.5 x 13 cm). Cover with paper mache (figure 3). Bend in half, then bend out about 1/2 inch (1.5 cm) on each end. Shape them to look like hands. Be sure to flare out the wrists; this will hold the rubber bands in place (figure 5). Let dry, apply gesso, and paint. Wax dip the hands and scrape off where the wrist area attaches to the arm.

10. Trim the poster board to 18 x 28 inches (46 x 72 cm), saving the scraps for the wings. Using hot glue, form a cone-shaped cylinder, leaving a 1-inch (2.5 cm) opening in the top and 9 inches (23 cm) at the bottom (figure 4). Trim the cone so it will

stand up. If you are making Genevieve, cover the cone with gold wrapping paper.

11. To make the dress, cut the fabric to 20 x 40 inches (51.5 x 102.5 cm). Glue a 1/4-inch (1 cm) hem on one 40-inch (102.5 cm) side (you can sew if you prefer). Gluing right sides together, join the 20-inch (51/5 cm) ends about 3/4 inches (2 cm) from the edge. Turn right side out and slip it over the cone. Gather up the raw edge at the top and secure it with a rubber band, leaving at least 1 inch (2.5) of fabric over the top of the cone. Apply glue to the inside top of the cone, then push the excess fabric down inside the cone. You can cut the rubber band off or cover it with ribbon for extra security.

12. For the arms, cut a piece of dress fabric 10 x 19 inches (25.5 x 8.5 cm) and fold it in half the long way, right sides together. Glue a seam at the raw edges, leaving about 3 inches (7.5 cm) open in the center (figure 5). Slip in the angel's hand (praying or two single hands); attach the wrist end to the end with the hands pointing toward the center. Leave about 1/2 inch (1.5 cm) of fabric over the wrist; wrap a rubber band around it. Pull the hands out through the opening, turning the fabric right side out. Add a little stuffing in the opening to give the arms fullness. Glue the opening shut.

13. To attach the head, put plenty of glue on the bottom of the neck and push it into the top of the cone.

14. Cut the wings out of posterboard (figure 6). For Angelena's wings cut out muslin 1/4 inch (1 cm) larger than the wing pattern. Cover the posterboard with muslin, fold over a 1/4-inch (1 cm) edge, and glue it on the back. Cut a piece of gold paper to cover the back of the wings. For Genevieve, paint the posterboard wings with gold fabric paint. Then attach the premade gold puffed wings.

15. Attach the arms at the center about 1 inch (2.5 cm) from the top back of the cone. Now glue on the wings on top of where you glued on the arms.

16. Decorate as you like with ribbon, lace, or gold cord. For Genevieve, you'll need to decorate the basket with flowers. The basket shown here contains mostly hydrangeas, delphinium, and amaranths. Arrange the flowers and glue them in place. Glue the hands to the basket.

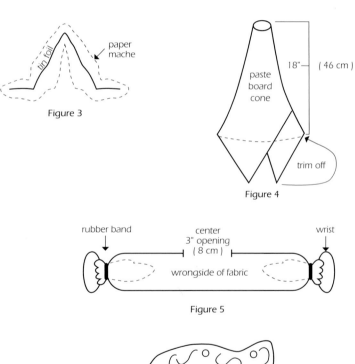

Figure 3

Figure 4

Figure 5

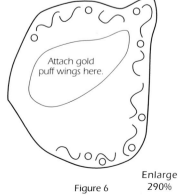

Figure 6

Enlarge 290%

Folk Art Angel

Designed by Dolly Lutz Morris to resemble an antique wood carving, this paper mache angel captures the timeless charm of early American crafts.

▸ *Music is well said to be the speech of angels.*

THOMAS CARLYLE

Designer:
Dolly Lutz Morris
Size: 3 x 9 inches
(7.5 x 23 cm)

Materials ▾

cardboard or posterboard

paper mache mix

6 inches (15.5 cm) stiff wire

acrylic paints in colors of your choice

spray sealer, matte finish

antiquing medium*

cellophane tape

cotton swabs

*brown stain mixed with paint thinner or
brown acrylic paint thinned with water makes
an excellent antiquing medium*

Tools ▾

wire cutters

scissors

metal nail file or sculpting tool

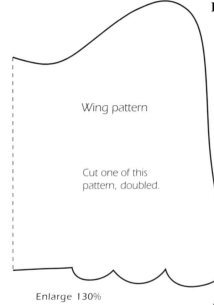

Wing pattern

*Cut one of this
pattern, doubled.*

fold

Enlarge 130%

Instructions ▾

1. Form the armature for the body of the angel by making a cone 8-1/2 inches (22 cm) tall and 2 inches (5 cm) at the base. Tape the cone together.

2. Bend a 6-inch (15.5 cm) length of wire in a v-shape. Insert the two ends of the v-shaped wire into the top of the cone and secure with tape. This forms the support for the neck and head.

3. Fold a small piece of cardboard and trace the wing pattern onto it. Cut out the wing and unfold. Attach the wings to the back of the cone with tape.

4. Mix your paper mache medium according to manufacturer's directions. Cover the cone with a 1/4-inch (1 cm) layer of paper mache, smoothing well with your fingers. Make the neck from a 1/2-inch-thick (1.5 cm) coil of paper mache and blend well into the cone. Add a 1-inch (2.5 cm) mache oval to the top of the neck, forming a rough head shape. Features will be added later.

5. Cover the wing fronts with a thin 1/8-inch (.5 cm) layer of mache and draw in the feather designs with the nail file.

6. Allow the project to dry before proceeding with the next steps.

7. Add more paper mache to the neck and smooth the surfaces until the neck is 3/4 inches (2 cm) wide.

8. Apply paper mache to the shoulder and chest areas, building up layers until the body is in correct proportions.

9. Apply paper mache layers to create the apron and robe. With your file, make straight vertical lines on the apron so that it resembles a wood carving. Design the bottom band of the apron, using the photograph as a guide.

10. Beneath the apron, on the robe, create a pleated look by pressing the file into the paper mache.

11. Apply mache to the back of the wings, again drawing feathers with your file.

12. Make two paper mache coils, 3-1/4 inches (8.5 cm) long and 1/2 inch (1.5 cm) thick, for the sleeves. Place the coils on the angel's shoulders and blend in with your fingers. Bend the sleeves to create the elbows and use your file to carve out the cuffs.

13. Fashion the angel's trumpet, attach it to the body, and blend well. Then redefine the trumpet with your file.

14. Make small paper mache balls for the hands. Place the hands over the trumpet and under the sleeves and blend well. Draw fingers on the hands with the file.

15. Now add the features to the face. Make a small rectangle for the forehead, a triangle for the nose, and tiny balls for the cheeks. Indent the eyes. Add a tiny ball for the chin and a rectangle above the chin for the lips. Use your file to carve the details on the lips. Wet a cotton swab and rub it over the facial features until the face is blended smooth.

16. Make the angel's hair, and blend and texture. Add a 1/2-inch (1.5 cm) ball to create a bun.

17. Allow your angel to dry completely, usually two to three days.

18. Paint the angel with acrylic paints thinned with water. Allow to dry.

19. Spray the figure with sealer and let it dry.

20. Apply the antiquing medium with a brush. With a smooth cotton cloth, wipe off the excess medium until you achieve the desired effect.

21. Apply two or three coats of sealer, letting each coat dry thoroughly.

Talented designers Jan Miles and Maggie Rotman, working with the imaginative direction of designer Susan Kinney, pooled their talents to decorate a bedroom. The transformation is indeed a transfiguration!

Instructions for the wall painting, pillows, and curtains appear on the following pages.

Angel With Doves

This extraordinary, luminous wall painting is the creation of Jan Miles. The inspiration for this mysterious angel was the memory of a chance encounter with a seemingly homeless stranger whose few words to her about love made a lasting impression. Perhaps Jan's compelling and personal expression can serve as inspiration for your own unique, celestial mural.

Designer: Jan Miles

Materials ▼

oil-based paints: 3 tones of blue paint—turquoise, Prussian blue, and pthalo blue; light golden yellow, golden orange, and creamy white

interference pigments mixed with acrylic emulsion: blue, violet, pearl, white, and copper*

glazing medium

metallic powders: gold, copper, and silver

premixed from Daniel Smith, 4150 First Ave. S., P.O. Box 84268, Seattle, WA 98124-5568, 1-800-426-6740.

Tools ▼

paintbrushes

rags

Instructions ▼

1. Apply a creamy white base coat and let dry.

2. Brush on a glaze of golden orange in random strokes similar to that of a color wash. Let dry.

3. Brush on thin washes of the different blues to help define the sky and cloud areas. Add deeper tones of blue to establish a sense of depth.

4. Randomly apply a series of metallic powders to accent the deep blue sky and create a sense of atmosphere.

5. Paint the angel and doves with the interference paint mixture. Seen from the angle of illumination, these semitransparent colors become extremely vibrant with metallic sheen.

6. Sand the surrounding walls and whitewash with cool to warming tones of white, orange, and yellow.

Designer: Maggie Rotman
Size: 18 x 24 inches (46 x 61.5 cm) per wing

Angel Wing Pillows

Designer Maggie Rotman created this pair of cloud-soft angel wings to protect you while you sleep.

Materials ▼

2 yards (133.5 cm) winter white cotton velvet 54 inches (138.5 cm) wide

1 spool heavy gold thread about the width of angel hair pasta

sewing thread to match velvet

1 yard (92.5 cm) muslin

pillow form or polyester fiberfill

stencil from angel curtain project on page 53

Tools ▼

Sewing machine equipment

Instructions ▼

1. Wash and dry the velvet unless you plan to dry clean it.

2. Use the stencil you made for the angel curtains on page x or follow steps 6 and 7. Lightly trace the section of angel wing onto the front side of each pillow (remember to reverse the design for the left pillow).

3. Back the wrong side of the velvet front with muslin.

4. Couch the gold thread over the lines of the design. A zigzag stitch works well to hold the thread in place.

5. On the muslin side of the fabric, slit a small hole on each section of the design (figure 1). Stuff with polyester fiberfill and stitch the opening together.

6. When each section of the design has been stuffed, place the two wrong sides of the velvet together and sew around the outer edge of the pillow form, leaving a 10-inch (25.5 cm) opening to turn the pillow right side out.

7. To complete, stuff the pillow with fiberfill and stitch the opening together.

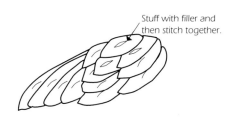

Stuff with filler and then stitch together.

Angel Wing Curtains

When sunlight filters through these gauzy curtains designed by Maggie Rotman, and the wind sets them fluttering, the room seems full of angels.

Designer: Maggie Rotman
Size: designed for windows 52 x 75 inches (133.5 x 192.5 cm)

Materials ▾

For two windows

38 yards (35 m) of 45-inch-wide (115.5 cm) unbleached muslin (the softest and finest you can find)

2 suspension rods for inner curtains

2 cafe rods 1/2 inch (1.5 cm) in diameter for outer curtains

shirring tape

3/4-inch (2 cm) plastic rings

50 x 75-inch (128 x 192.5 cm) roll of brown manilla paper for stencil; may be pieced from 36-inch (92.5 cm) roll

plastic sheeting

self-sealing pad or cardboard 50 x 75 inches (128 x 192.5 cm)

fabric paint—1 fl. oz. (3 cl) each: pearl, white metallic, crimson, light yellow, and light red

2 fl. oz. (6 cl) acrylic interference gold

4 fl. oz. (12 cl) pearl white in bottle with painting tip

Tools ▾

1-1/2- or 3/4-inch (4 cm or 2 cm) stencil brush

1-inch (2.5 cm) paintbrush

sewing machine equipment

sharp craft knife

Instructions ▾

1. Wash, dry, and iron the muslin. Cut it into lengths as follows:

    6 panels 74-inches-long (190 cm)

    8 panels 78-inches-long (200 cm)

Inner curtains

2. Cut two of the 74-inch (190 cm) panels in half lengthwise. Join one to each of the remaining full-width panels along the long edges (figure 1). You now have four panels 67 x 74 inches (172 x 190 cm). You can trim selvedges on the vertical edges and make a narrow seam if you wish.

3. Make two 2-1/2-inch (6.5 cm) folds at the top and two 2-inch (5 cm) folds at the bottom of each of these panels. Stitch on the seam edge.

4. At the top of each panel make an additional row of stitching 1 inch (2.5 cm) above the hem edge to create a rod pocket (figure 2).

Outer curtains (angel wing panels)

5. Join pairs of 78-inch (200 cm) panels together. This will give you four panels 78 x 90 inches (200 cm x 231 cm).

6. Draw a simplified version of figure 3 (see figure 4) onto the manilla paper the width of half the outer curtain—45 x 78 inches (115.5 x 200 cm). Place the paper on a surface with a self-sealing pad or on a sheet of cardboard. Use a sharp craft knife to make a stencil from the drawing. Make the cut line about 1/4-inch-wide (1 cm) on average. Remember to leave tabs to hold the stencil together. The stencil will be very large to handle in one piece; you may want to cut it in half at an appropriate place in the design.

7. Cover your work surface with plastic sheeting. Anchor the fabric and the stencil on the work surface with weights or pins. Using the stencil brush and interference gold, stencil the design on each panel, remembering to reverse two of the panels to get a right and left curtain.

8. When the outline is dry, you are ready to apply the color. Mix the base color from the light yellow, light red, and pearl white to achieve a pale orange. Take some of this and water it down to a very watery wash. Paint each feather in the design with this wash. As you get to the tip of the feather add stronger color right from the undiluted paint, and include a little of the crimson red at the very tip (figure 4). (Practice this first on a scrap of fabric until you get the right color intensity. It looks very different when the fabric is wet; it lightens up considerably when dry.) It's best to let the curtain dry on your work surface. If time is an issue, lift the painted curtain carefully, avoid any dragging motion so that paint does not get on the unpainted surface, and hang it up to dry.

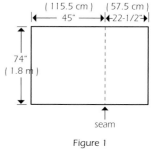

(115.5 cm)   (57.5 cm)

45"   22-1/2"

74" (1.8 m)

seam

Figure 1

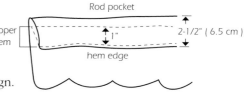

Rod pocket

upper hem

1"

hem edge

2-1/2" (6.5 cm)

Figure 2

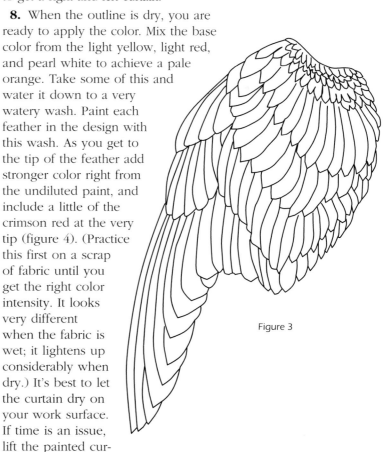

Figure 3

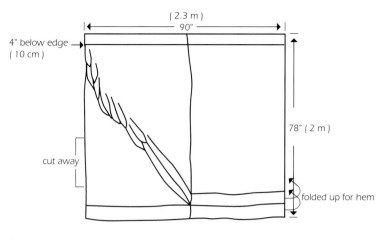

Figure 4

9. When dry, place a bead of the pearl fabric paint (with the painting nozzle) along the shaped edge of the curtain; when this has hardened, cut away the excess fabric at the edge.

10. Fold 2 inches (5 cm) of fabric at the top of the curtain and attach the shirring tape. Sew 3/4-inch-diameter (2 cm) plastic rings at 5-6-inch (13-16 cm) intervals along the tape, and gather it to fit your window. This allows the curtains to be drawn smoothly. If this is not an issue, just make a pocket as for the inner curtains.

11. To finish, make a 2-inch (5 cm) hem on the bottom of each curtain.

The Necessary Angel

Ellen Wolfe and her mother, Ruth Siegel, are making their own special contribution to the upsurge of interest in angels. They own and operate The Necessary Angel in Brookline Village and Edgartown, Massachusetts, delightful shops that sell only high quality, handcrafted angels. Ellen, who had been contemplating opening a crafts gallery, landed on the idea of this shop overnight. She literally woke up and said "It's angels!"

She particularly wanted to focus on multicultural angels to reflect the diverse nature of people's spiritual backgrounds. The angels in her shop represent a wide array of materials, techniques, and styles. What they share are the shop owners' respect for the universality of angels. Here's a list of a few of the many large and small cities around the country that feature angel shops: Portland, Oregon; Asheville, North Carolina; Birmingham, Alabama; Los Gatos, California; Norcross, Georgia; Edina, Minnesota; and Maui, Hawaii.

The polymer clay angel featured here is by Susan Hyde, one of the many talented artists whose celestial work can be purchased at The Necessary Angel. Photo: Roger Schriber.

Angel Quilt

The genesis of this fanciful quilt was designer Dort Lee's strategy to break the ice between her shy, quiet nine-year-old daughter, Anna, and an equally shy and nontalkative friend-to-be, Mariah. Each girl made three angels, mom made the other two and designed a quilt to proudly show them off.

Designer: Dort Lee
Size: 4 x 4 feet (123.5 cm x 123.5 cm)

Materials ▾

1-1/2 yards (138.5 cm) fabric for background
fabric scraps
ribbons
lace
glitter
sequins
other notions
fabric drawing pens
invisible thread
craft glue

Tools ▾

scissors
sewing machine equipment

Instructions ▾

1. Cut fabric squares of different sizes for the background.

2. Freehand cut (or draw first and then cut) the angels.

3. Glue them to the background fabric.

4. Draw in the faces.

5. Decorate the angels and the backgrounds with glitter, ribbons, buttons, etc. In general, the more you add, the better.

6. Sew the angels to the background using a zigzag stitch and invisible thread.

7. Proceed with the construction of a quilt of your own design. Or you can incorporate the angel squares into a purchased quilt pattern. Another very simple option: cut around the angels and appliqué them onto a purchased quilt or comforter.

Appliqued Angel Pillow

A quartet of elegant angels serenades all those who can hear the heavenly melody. Designer Carol Parks appliquéd the angels against a velvet, star-studded sky.

Designer: Carol Parks
Size: 14 inches (36 cm) square

Materials ▾

14-inch (36 cm) pillow form

3/8 yard (34.5 cm) dark blue cotton velvet for central panel

1/2 yard (46 cm) navy/gold stars cotton print for outer border and back

1/2 yard (46 cm) ivory/gold stars cotton print for inner border

cotton scraps for appliqué

unbleached muslin scraps for angels' robes

1-5/8 yards (138 cm) piping cord with welt

crisp iron-on backing material for central panel

paper-backed transfer web for appliqués

metallic gold thread and sewing thread to match appliqués

Tools ▾

hand sewing and sewing machine equipment

special sewing machine needle designed for use with metallic threads

clear appliqué presser foot (optional)

water-soluble fabric-marking pencil in white

carpenter's square, rotary cutter, and mat

sharp craft knife

Instructions ▾

1. Cut one 11-1/2 x 11-1/2-inch (29.5 x 29.5 cm) velvet square for the central panel. Cut one 12-1/2 x 12-1/2-inch (32 x 32 cm) ivory/gold stars print for the inner border. Cut two 15 x 15-inch (38.5 x 38.5 cm) squares of navy/gold stars print for the outer border and the back.

2. Cut the iron-on backing 14 x 14 inches (36 x 36 cm). Center it on the wrong side of the velvet with 1/2 inch (1.5 cm) all around, and fuse following manufacturer's instructions.

3. Press the transfer web to the wrong side of the fabrics to be used for appliqué.

4. Trace or photocopy the appliqué patterns. Cut out the pieces and place them upside down on the paper-backed fabric pieces. Draw around the figures and cut them out with a sharp craft knife.

5. Remove the paper backing from the appliqué pieces and arrange them on the velvet panel, keeping within 1 inch (2.5 cm) of the outer edge and using the photo as a guide. Press lightly to hold them in

place, then fuse according to manufacturer's instructions.

6. Using a narrow, open zigzag stitch, stitch around the appliqués. An appliqué presser foot is helpful. Pull thread ends to the wrong side and leave them fairly long.

7. Change to gold metallic thread (and special needle) and embellish the angels' robes, using the photo as a guide. Work the stars. Sew slowly with metallic thread; it may be necessary to slightly loosen the upper tension.

8. Press under the seam allowances on the panel. Center it on the ivory/gold stars fabric and topstitch in place with gold thread, sewing very close to the folded edges.

9. Change to a regular needle and thread. Press under the seam allowances on the ivory/gold stars fabric (inner border piece) and stitch to the navy/gold stars piece in the same way.

10. Stitch the piping to the right side of the cover, stitching exactly on the seam line of the fabric. Use a zipper foot or piping foot. Clip through the welt at the corners to round them smoothly.

11. Sew the cover front to back with the right sides together, stitching on the piping stitching line. Leave most of one side open.

12. Insert the pillow and stitch the opening by hand.

Hair

Face

Horn

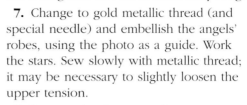

Gown

Wing

Enlarge all pattern pieces 215%

▶ *Silently one by one, in the infinite meadows of heaven*

Blossomed the lovely stars, the forget-me-nots of angels.

Henry Wadsworth Longfellow

Cherubs and Stars Pillow

Designer Catherine Reurs created this captivating celestial canvas, suitable for needlepoint or counted cross-stitch.

Designer: Catherine Reurs
Size: 14 x 12 inches (36 x 31 cm)

Materials ▾

18 x 20-inch (46 x 51.5 cm) needlepoint
  canvas, 12 mesh or

19 x 22-inch (48.5 x 56.5 cm) black or
  navy Aida cloth, 14 count

masking tape

gold and blue braid

3-ply tapestry wool or embroidery floss

Tools ▾

scissors

three #18 tapestry needles

Instructions ▾

Needlepoint

Note: On the pattern, one square equals
one stitch. The symbol inside the square
denotes the color (see key to chart). You
may use the basketweave or the continental
stitch. The finished size is 12 x 14 inches.

1. Cover raw edges of the canvas with
masking tape to prevent unraveling.

2. Work all stitches with two plys of the
three-ply wool.

3. Start in the center or at one corner or a
side. Stitch the details and the design first,
then fill in the background. Work lighter
colors first whenever possible; this keeps
the darker wool from catching on the
lighter threads and distorting their color.
Keep your stitch tension as uniform as
possible.

4. When you come to the end of a strand,
weave the remaining 1 inch (2.5 cm)
through the back of the canvas, across and
under the same color stitches. This will
give you a neat, finished back.

5. Follow the normal method of making a
pillow, using a suitably sturdy material
such as velvet or velveteen. The blue and
gold cording will add a touch of elegance
to your finished piece.

Counted Cross-stitch

1. Select navy blue or black Aida fabric to
give you the best background color. The
fabric should measure 19 x 22 inches (48.5
x 56.6 cm).

2. Tape the edges of the fabric with masking tape to prevent unraveling.

3. Using the tapestry needle and three
strands of embroidery floss, begin in the
middle of the canvas and work your way
to the edges.

4. Hide your loose strands by weaving
them under and across similarly colored
stitches on the back of the cloth.

5. Follow the normal method of making a
pillow, or block and frame the finished
piece as a sampler.

KEY TO CHART

	COLORS	PATERNAYAN WOOL #	WOOL AMOUNT	DMC FLOSS #	ANCHOR FLOSS #
	navy blue	571	135 yds (125 m)	336	150
	purple	330	10 yds (9.25 m)	550	112
	dk yellow	711	15 yds (13.9 m)	972	298
	lt yellow	772	15 yds (13.9 m)	444	290
	dk orange	832	10 yds (9.25 m)	922	1003
	md orange	833	10 yds (9.25 m)	722	323
	lt orange	834	10 yds (9.25 m)	758	9575
	pale orange	846	18 yds (16.65 m)	950	4146
	gold metallic	—	7 yds (6.75 m)	gold metallic	gold metallic

Enlarge 124%

Enlarge 124%

Enlarge 124%

Enlarge 124%

Blue Angel

This small wall hanging, designed and hooked by Jeanne Fallier, shimmers with the ethereal beauty and mystery long associated with angels. Hooked on very fine linen with hand-dyed wools, the angel appears to be floating in the sky.

Designer: Jeanne H. Fallier

Size: 17 x 20 inches (44 x 51 cm)

Materials ▾

#3 blade strips of the following:

  2 swatches of "angel blue" for wings and robe*

  1 yard solid color for sky

  small amounts of other colors

1 spool metallic gold thread

17 x 20-inch piece of very fine linen or burlap

17 x 20-inch piece of muslin for backing

20-inch curtain rod

Yarn for wings and robe: Maryanne Lincoln, 139 Park Street, Wrentham, Massachusetts 02093, (617) 384-8188.

Tools ▾

rug hooking equipment

Instructions ▾

1. Gather all your strips (cut on the narrowest blade setting). The designer hand-dyed the wool, but you can work with predyed strips in shaded color groupings.

2. Hook the wings with gradation swatches of blue. Begin the wings lightest at the head or halo and deepen the color as they sweep outward, using the full range of blue values.

3. The colors in the robe range from pale blue to violet, with the deeper hues in the shadows of the skirt folds at the bottom.

4. For the halo, begin with a pale yellow on the innermost circle, and spread out in deeper tones of gold. The medium and darker golds of the swatch were used for the sash, too.

5. For the face use a soft pinkish tone. Try a slight blush color for the cheekbone, surrounded by the lightest values running to the chin, slightly deeper shadows from the nose and under the lip, and even deeper shadows outlining the chin and jaw to separate the face from the neck. On the hairline, try a shading just a touch deeper than the lightest value of the forehead.

6. Use a soft rose red for the mouth. For the hands, try a slightly deeper pink than the face.

7. Add a few leaves in her floral crown. After finishing the halo, crown, and sash with the yellow and gold swatches, add a few tiny loops of gold metallic thread to each.

8. Accent the navy sky with lighter value blue to indicate clouds. With gold threads, dot the night sky here and there with a few minute sparkling stars.

9. Keep the border colors muted so as not to compete with the angel's face.

10. Finish the piece with muslin lining. Stitch a pocket at the top for the curtain rod; leave the bottom open to allow air in and dust out.

Enlarge 171%. Use 1/2-inch-square graph paper.

Guardian Angel Applique Banner

Designer Mary Parker took the same magnificent angel she designed for a vest and made it bigger, blue, and very, very gold so it would catch the eye and the wind.

Materials ▾

1-1/4 yards (115.5 cm) fabric for banner background

1/2 yard (46 cm) solid-gold-colored fabric for wings and halo

1/8 yard (11.5 cm) solid-silver-colored fabric

1 spool gold metallic thread

1 spool silver metallic thread

1/2 yard (46 cm) brocade for dress

1 spool rayon or metallic thread to match brocade

10 yards (9.25 m) gold soutache braid for hair

1 spool invisible nylon thread

Designer: Mary S. Parker
Size: 30 x 40 inches (77 x 102.5 cm)

polyester fiberfill

weights for bottom hem of banner (optional)

Tools ▾

Sewing machine with teflon-coated foot

hand sewing and sewing machine equipment

You will find the pattern for this angel on page 105.

Angels at Biltmore Estate

Christmas, with all it glorious delights, takes on a grand scale at the Biltmore House, the largest privately owned home in America. In fact, Biltmore Estate first opened in 1895 for a Christmas eve celebration. Many Christmas traditions originated in America around that time: bringing a tree into the home to decorate, writing and singing carols, and focusing on Santa Claus. Christmas is celebrated at Biltmore House from mid-November through the end of December, with decorations in rooms throughout the house.

These photographs were taken in the library where the theme of angels ties in with the cherub-adorned ceiling painting created by the 18th century Italian artist, Giovanni Pellegrini. Pictured here is a tree bedecked with more than 100 angels and one especially luminous seraphim, poised on the mantel.

Mosaic Angels Frame

The haunting angels that ring this frame, created by Susan Kinney, are based on those
that appear on the painted ceiling of the Church of Debre Berhan in Ethiopia.

Designer: Susan Kinney
Size: 5 x 7 inches (13 x 18 cm)

Materials ▾

1 block each of black, white, and flesh-colored polymer clay

1/2 block each of brown, red, and gold polymer clay

metal or wooden picture frame with flat or rounded edges

fine-grit sandpaper

Tools ▾

oven or toaster oven

slicing blade or pasta machine

brayer

food processor (used for clay only)

Instructions ▾

1. Knead all the clay until it is the same consistency.

2. Cut the flesh-colored clay in half, and reserve half for a later step.

3. Mix a pea-sized ball of black with a fourth of the flesh-colored clay. Use this shadowflesh to form the simple face cane, using the photograph as a guide. Circle two-thirds of the face with a black sheet of hair, and underline the chin area with a thin sheet of black.

4. For the halo, make bull's-eyes by wrapping red snakes with dark gold. Wrap the red and gold coil with a very thin layer of black. Arrange the three-tiered halo onto the face cane.

5. Form the wing tips by making a bull's-eye coil of white wrapped with brown. Divide the coil into four pieces. Graduate the coils in size by rolling the second piece smaller than the first, and so on. Arrange the coils from large to small to form a long triangle. Wrap the triangle cane with a thin sheet of black.

6. Arrange the wing tip triangles around the halo.

7. Using a chopping motion and your slicing blade (or a food processor with a shredder blade), chop and blend together the leftover shadowflesh, the remaining flesh color, and several 1/2-inch (1.75 cm) balls of red and black. This clay mixture is the granitelike color you'll use for the frame base and the face cane filler.

8. Pack coils of the granite clay in between the wing tips of the angel face until you have filled out the entire face cane into a circle.

9. Allow the cane to rest overnight.

10. Place the cane between your palms and gently roll it, both to compress and to elongate the coils. Reduce the cane to whatever size your frame surface is. The cane in the photograph was about 1 inch (2.5 cm) in diameter. You will not need the whole cane; use the leftover cane for pins, earrings, buttons, or beads.

11. Roll out sheets of granite color and press onto the frame as smoothly as possible. Use your brayer to roll over the frame, gently pressing the clay onto the surface.

12. Cut the face cane into very thin slices and arrange the slices in a pleasing manner around the frame on top of the granite. Blend the faces into the granite, making the finish as smooth as possible.

13. Round off the edges and trim any excess from around the frame.

14. Bake the frame, being sure to follow the manufacturer's instructions for the polymer clay you're using. Allow the frame to cool completely.

15. When the frame is cool, lightly sand it.

16. You may finish with a spray sealer if you wish.

▶ *We are like children, who stand in need of masters to enlighten us and direct us; and God has provided for this, by appointing his angels to be our teachers and guides.*

Saint Thomas Aquinas

► *For He shall give His angels charge over thee, to keep thee in all thy ways. They shall bear thee up in their hands, lest thou dash thy foot against a stone.*

PSALM 91:11–12

Designer: Terry Taylor
Size: 6 inches (15.5 cm)

Mosaic Cherub

Pique-assiette or shard art *describes a 19th century craft that uses china and other ceramic items to floridly decorate otherwise ordinary objects. Designer Terry Taylor enjoys how this craft, especially popular in the Victorian era, can transform a plain concrete angel into something quite heavenly.*

Materials ▾

concrete garden cherub*

4–8 inexpensive china plates in your choice of colors

tile mortar supplies

interior/exterior grade floor grout

large plastic containers

old towel

scrap of soft cloth

foam packaging material (sheet type)

rubber gloves

masking tape

safety glasses

sheet plastic or garbage bags to cover work area

available at most garden shops or concrete ornament suppliers

Tools ▾

hammer

tile nippers

small plastic artist's trowel/palette knife

Instructions ▾

1. Amass your crockery! Look for plates with flattened rims—they give more usable shards. Buy more than you think you will need. You can always get a break (no pun intended) in price by pointing out the chips and cracks!

2. Wrap the plates in a folded towel. Protect your eyes with safety glasses. Give the plates a good whack with a hammer. Open the towel and check the size of the pieces. Rewrap and whack again.

3. Use tile nippers to break the shards into small, workable sizes; 1/2-inch (1.5 cm) squares are a good start. Sort the shards into color piles for quick access.

4. Using about 1/3 to 1/2 cup (80-120 ml) of water, mix the dry tile mortar according to manufacturer's directions. Mix to the consistency of stiff mashed potatoes; this makes it easier to hold the shards on curved surfaces.

5. Using the small trowel, coat the front of the wings with about an 1/8-inch-thick (.5 cm) layer of mortar.

6. Working from the outside edge, put the shards in place close to one another, but leave space between them for the grout. If the mortar oozes up, use the trowel to scrape off the excess. Nip the shards to fit as necessary.

7. Let the shards set up for a couple of hours, preferably overnight.

8. Repeat steps 4 - 7 on the back side of the wings.

9. Mask the cherub's body and face with tape to prevent staining in the next steps.

10. Cut the foam packaging material into 3- or 4-inch (7.5-10.5 cm) squares and set them aside.

11. Mix the grout according manufacturer's directions. Again, use about 1/2 cup (120 ml) of water. Use a small trowel to coat the entire wing surface with grout. Use the foam squares to spread it evenly into all the crevices. Continue "scrubbing" the surface with the foam squares until the shards are clearly visible. Allow the grout to set up according to the manufacturer's directions; wipe clean with damp sponge to dissolve grout haze on the shards.

12. Polish the shards with a soft cloth.

13. Allow the grout to cure for a couple of days. Perch the cherub in your garden. Be sure to protect it from winter's freeze and thaw.

14. Options: gild the body with exterior gold enamel; for an indoor angel, use wall grout.

Table Runner

Mary Parker's ingenious design is certain to enhance any dinner party all year 'round.

Designer: Mary Parker
Size: 10 x 72 inches (26 x 183 cm)

Materials ▾

fashion fabric 12 inches (31 cm) wide and
20 inches (51.5 cm) longer than length
of table

1 spool regular sewing thread to match
fashion fabric

fusible polyester fleece 10 inches (25.5 cm)
wide and 18 inches (46 cm) longer than
length of table

1 spool decorative heavy-weight rayon
thread

tissue or pattern paper to serve as pattern
transfer

Tools ▾

hand sewing and sewing machine equipment

bobbin adjusted to accommodate heavier-
weight thread

needle threader (useful for getting the
heavy decorative thread to go through
the eye of the hand sewing needle)

dark color of iron-on transfer pen

Instructions ▾

1. Cut the fabric for the runner.

2. Cut a piece of polyester fleece 10
inches (25.5 cm) wide and 2 inches (5 cm)
shorter than the length of fabric. (In step 9
you will use this piece of fleece as a pattern to cut out the bottom piece of the
runner.)

3. Fuse the fleece to the wrong side of
the top of the runner, leaving a 1-inch (2.5
cm) fabric border around the perimeter of
the fleece.

4. Planning your design: a) The template
has been designed so that the angels (see
patterns) can be connected to each other
at their halos, hems, or wing tips. This
enables their outlines to be stitched in several long, continuous passes from one end
of the runner to the other, minimizing the
amount of knot tying to be done to secure
the decorative thread. b) The angels can
be formed horizontally or vertically. On a
group of angels which are linked horizontally like the one used on the outer edges
of the runner, stitching would begin at one
end and continue across the top halves of
each of the joined angels to the other end
of the runner. Often, a pivot can be made
at the far end of the runner, and the same
stitching continued back to complete the
bottom halves of each of the angels until

you have returned to the original starting point. On a group of angels that
are linked vertically like the one used
in the center, begin to stitch at one
end of the runner, down the left-hand
side of the first angel; then, switch to
the right-hand side. Continue in
this manner to the end of the
design. Often, a pivot can be
made at the far end, and the
same stitching continued back
alternating left and right to
complete the rest of the design.
If this is not possible, return to
the other end of the runner and
stitch down the right-hand side
of the first angel, switching to
the left-hand side of the next
angel. Continue in this manner until
you have reached the bottom of the
design. c) Considering these stitching
options, determine how you would like
to position the angels.
Usually your design will
consist of a panel that is
repeated every few feet.
You may find it helpful
to make a full-size draft
of this panel on tissue
paper, make several photo-
copies, and tape them
together to create a full-size
draft to enable you to see
exactly how your finished
product will look.

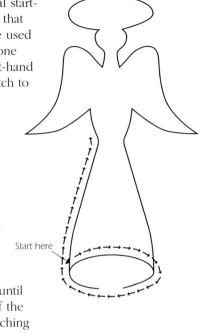

Start here

Enlarge 123%

5. Making a transfer pattern:
a) Once you have final-
ized your design, go over
your pencil trac-
ings with a dark
iron-on transfer pen
to mark the design
so it can be trans-
ferred. b) Transfer
the design to the
fusible fleece side of the runner
according to the manufacturer's direction
for iron-on transfer pen.

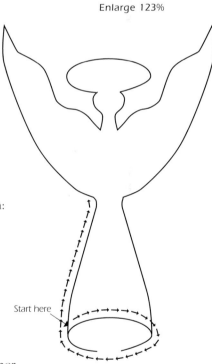

Start here

6. Preparing your machine: a) You will
be stitching the decorative pattern with the
fusible fleece side of the runner facing
upwards and the fashion fabric side of the
runner against your feed dogs. You will
therefore wind the decorative rayon thread
onto your bobbin, rather than threading it
through your needle. You will probably
wish to fill several bobbins before beginning to stitch on your design so that you

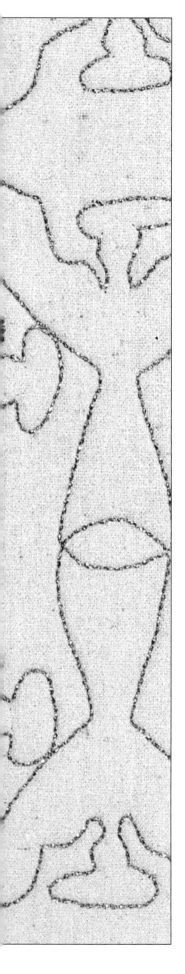

do not have to take your needle thread out to refill your bobbin during your stitching. b) If you do not have a special bobbin case designed to accommodate heavier-weight thread, you will need to adjust your bobbin case. Loosen the bobbin tension until the decorative thread flows with the same degree of resistance that regular thread normally exhibits. Load the bobbin and bobbin case into your sewing machine. c) Thread the needle of your machine with thread that matches your fashion fabric. You will probably need to loosen your needle tension so that the needle thread will be pulled almost all the way through to the fashion fabric.

7. Stitching the design: a) Bring your bobbin thread up through the feed-dogs and pull enough bobbin thread through to create at least a 5-inch tail. (You will need this much slack to thread the tail through a hand sewing needle in order to pull it through to the fusible fleece side and tie it off.) b) Make sure you hold the ends of both the bobbin thread and the needle thread as you start to stitch so that the tail of the bobbin thread does not get caught in your stitching. c) You will have less chance of the tail of bobbin thread accidently getting caught in your stitching if you pull it through to the fusible fleece side of your design as soon as you possibly can. Once you have stitched several inches away from your starting point, pause in your machine stitching, leaving your sewing machine needle in the down position so that it will hold your fabric in place. Thread the tail of the bobbin thread through a hand sewing needle (using a needle threader if necessary) in order to bring it through to the fusible fleece side. Then tie a square knot with the needle thread tail and the bobbin tail. You can trim the tail of thread after you have tied the knot, but always leave at least 1 inch (3 cm). d) Stitch as much of the design as possible before cutting off your threads and starting a new line of stitching. Always remember to leave at least a 5-inch (13 cm) tail on your bobbin thread before cutting it off. Bring the tail of the bobbin thread through the fusible fleece side, knot, and trim, before beginning another line of stitching.

8. Repairing imperfections: a) After you have sewn your entire design, make sure that you have brought all your bobbin threads through to the fusible fleece side and tied a square knot with them and the needle thread. Turn your runner over to the fashion fabric side and look for noticeable imperfections. b) You can correct areas of stitching by cutting the decorative rayon thread and the regular sewing thread once in the center of the problem area. Carefully pull out both the decorative rayon thread and the regular sewing thread, working from both sides of the cut far enough back to create enough slack so that the decorative rayon thread can be threaded through a needle, brought to the fusible fleece side of the runner, and tied off in a square knot with the regular sewing thread. c) Resew the problem area, being sure to leave thread tails at least 5 inches (13 cm) long at the beginning and ending of your stitching so that you can pull the decorative rayon thread through to the fusible fleece side and knot it off.

9. Take out your bobbin with the decorative rayon thread and replace it with a bobbin wound with regular sewing thread that matches your fashion fabric. Stitch around the perimeter of the runner, turning the fashion fabric under 1/4 inch (1 cm) toward the wrong side of the fashion fabric on all sides. Then form a hem by pressing the entire remaining width of fashion fabric that does not have the polyester fleece fused to it toward the polyester fleece side of the runner. (You should have approximately a 3/4-inch (2 cm) width pressed under all the way around your runner). Set the top of the runner aside.

10. Take the bottom of the runner that you cut out in step 2 and stitch around its perimeter, turning the edge under 1/2 inch (1.5 cm) toward the wrong side of the fashion fabric all the way around. Place the top and the bottom of the runner with wrong sides together. Pin in place so that the bottom piece is centered on the underside of the top piece. You should not be able to see anything but fashion fabric on the underside of the runner.

11. Secure the top and bottom of the runner together by one of the following methods:

a) Use a fusible web to bond the top and bottom pieces of the runner together, or

b) Hand stitch the top and bottom pieces of the runner together.

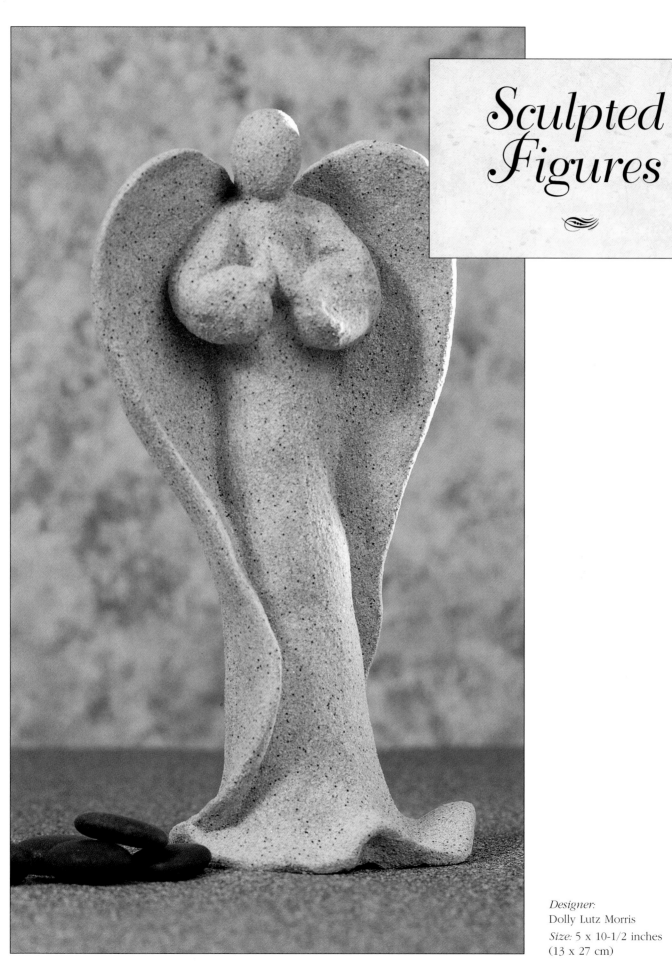

Sculpted Figures

Designer:
Dolly Lutz Morris
Size: 5 x 10-1/2 inches
(13 x 27 cm)

Peace Angel

Elegance and serenity are captured in this sculpture by Dolly Lutz Morris, who uses this angel in her daily meditations. Make this angel as large or small as you wish, just keep it proportional.

► *Where there's peace on earth, there are angels in the heavens.*

ANON.

Materials ▾

paper mache mix
posterboard
tape
granite-look spray paint
acrylic gesso
fine grit wet/dry sandpaper

Tools ▾

scissors
metal nail file
paintbrushes

Instructions ▾

1. Using posterboard, make a cone 10 inches (25.5 cm) high with a base of 2-1/2 inches (6.5 cm). Tape the cone together.

2. Cut a 5 x 9-inch (13 x 23 cm) heart from posterboard for the wings.

3. Tape the wings to the cone with wing tops even with the top of the cone. Bend the sides of the wings forward to look graceful and flowing.

4. Cover the entire figure with a 1/4-inch (1 cm) layer of paper mache, smoothing and blending well with your fingertips.

5. Add a 1-inch (2.5 cm) paper mache head to the top of the figure and blend this layer over the shoulders and torso to form a smooth figure. Allow the angel to dry.

6. Add another thin layer of paper mache on the wing edges to enhance the forward curves; blend until smooth.

7. To make the flowing gown, add the paper mache to the bottom of the wings and base. Curve the wing edges in gracefully, and lift up the gown edges with your nail file to suggest ruffles. Again, blend well.

8. Make two coils, 1 x 2-1/4 inches (2.5 x 6 cm) each, for arms, tapering the coils at the shoulders. Bend at the elbows and attach to the angel. Blend.

9. For the hands, work a 1/4-inch (1 cm) ball into an oval shape and place it between the sleeves and blend. Allow the figure to dry thoroughly, about two or three days, depending on the weather and humidity.

10. Lightly sand the figure two or three times.

11. Paint the angel with acrylic gesso; this will smooth and strengthen the figure.

12. Finish with two coats of granite-look paint, drying thoroughly between coats.

Rozelle

*After nights of deep thought, designer Diane Kuebitz's six-year-old son Edward
named this angel "Rozelle." No doubt the angel's whimsical nature spoke to
Edward (and perhaps there's a little bit of the child in Rozelle).*

▶ *An angel can
illumine the
thought and
mind of man
by strengthening
the power of
vision, and by
bringing within
his reach some
truth which the
angel himself
contemplates.*

SAINT THOMAS AQUINAS

Designer: Diane C. Kuebitz
Size: 8 inches (20.5 cm)

Materials ▾

polymer clay: flesh, gold, white, yellow, and purple*

acrylic paints: green, black, white, gold glitter, and clear glitter

pink chalk

pencil

baking sheet

aluminum foil

toothpicks

hot glue

less than one block of each color

Tools ▾

sculpting tools, sharp and blunt

short nail with 1/8-inch-wide (.5 cm) head

rolling pin or pasta machine

sharp knife

fine-tipped paintbrush

glue gun

Instructions ▾

1. *Armature:* a) Shape the aluminum foil into a cone 6 - 7 inches (15.5 - 18 cm) tall with a 2-inch-wide base. Insert a toothpick into the top. Flatten a 2-inch (5 cm) ball of purple or white clay into an 1/8-inch-thick (.5 cm) pancake. Place the foil cone in the center of the pancake and shape the sides of the clay around the bottom of the foil. b) Roll a 3/4-inch (2 cm) ball of white into an egg shape and press the small end onto the toothpick. Use your thumb to indent the face side of the egg. Wrap a small strip of clay around the neck and press firmly into place. Bake at 225 degrees Fahrenheit for 45 minutes.

2. *Head:* Roll a 3/4-inch (2 cm) ball of flesh and press it into the face indentation. Flatten another 3/4-inch (2 cm) ball into a 1-1/4-inch-wide (3 cm) pancake; use it to cover the neck and the back and top of the head. Use your thumbs to smooth the seams. Shape a chin.

3. *Face:* With a sharp tool, draw in the mouth. To shape the lips, roll two 3/8-inch (1.25 cm) balls of flesh and form each into a triangle; then flatten them and use a blunt tool to indent the middle of the upper lip. Place the lips over the mouth line.

4. *Cheeks:* Roll two 1/2-inch (1.5 cm) balls of flesh into comma shapes and flatten them slightly. Place them onto the face so that the inner curve of each comma almost

▶ *In heaven an angel is nobody in particular.*

GEORGE BERNARD SHAW

touches the lip corners. Gently smudge with your thumbs to blend the seam to the bottom of the chin. Blend the outer cheeks edges into the head. Indent the eye sockets.

5. *Nose:* Roll a 1/2-inch (1.5 cm) ball of flesh into a short cone and position it onto the face. Blend the top of the nose into the forehead.

6. *Eyes:* Make two 1/8-inch (.5 cm) balls of white and bake for 15 minutes at 225 degrees Fahrenheit. Press the baked eyes into the sockets. Use the pointed end of the toothpick to make tear ducts. Roll four tiny snake-shaped pieces of flesh for the eyelids and press them on the top and bottom of the eyes.

7. *Gown:* Flatten a 3-inch (7.5 cm) ball of purple into a pancake and use the rolling pin or pasta machine to make a large, flat sheet 1/16-inch (.25 cm) thick. Cut a 4-1/2 x 8-inch (11.5 x 20.5 cm) rectangle from the sheet. Press the cut edges against your palms to round them, form a tube, and slip it over the angel's head, with the seam at the back. Gather the gown around the neck, pressing the folds to secure them. Cut out the collar pieces and press to the gown. Cut a piece for the ruffles, press it on to the bottom of the gown, and scallop the edges.

8. *Sleeves:* Roll a 3/16 x 1-1/2-inch (1.25 x 4 cm) cylinder of purple. Insert the end of a pencil 3/4 inch (2 cm) into one end. Hold the sleeve with one hand and roll the pencil back and forth with the other. Bend the sleeve at the elbow and press both sleeves onto the shoulders.

9. *Hair:* Flatten half a block of yellow to a 1/8-inch (.5 cm) thickness, slice into 1/8-inch (.5 cm) strips, and connect them to her head at the top. gently twisting each strand.

10. *Halo and wand:* Cover a toothpick with gold. Shape a star and connect it to the wand. Roll out a 1/2-inch-thick (1.5 cm) thick snake for a halo.

11. *Hands:* Roll a 1/2-inch (1.5 cm) ball of flesh and shape the hands; use the sharp tool to make wrinkles in the knuckles and the nail head to make fingernails.

12. *Wings:* Flatten white into the desired shape. Roll 1/8-inch (.5 cm) balls of white and blend them into one another in brick formation. Bake at 225 degrees Fahrenheit for 1–2 hours, checking them every half hour.

13. After the wings have cooled, paint them with clear glitter. Use gold glitter on the ruffle, wand, and halo. Paint the eyes. Gently brush the pink chalk on her cheeks.

14. Hot glue the wings to her back.

Seashell Angel Mirror

This angel, designed by Carol Weyrauch, looks delicate and opalescent, as if she just emerged from a celestial sea.

Designer: Carol Weyrauch
Size: 3-1/2 x 4-1/2 inches (9 x 11.5 cm)

Materials ▾

2 blocks white polymer clay
seashells
doll or other face to be used as a mold
acrylic mirror
craft glue
scrap of fabric
scrap of satin ribbon

Tools ▾

oven or toaster oven
baking sheet
rolling pin
sharp knife
punch
scroll saw

Instructions ▾

1. To create the base for the mirror, roll the clay fairly thin and cut the desired shape. Cut the area where the mirror will be placed.

2. To create a mold for the clay face, make a ball of clay about twice as large as the doll, ornament, or sculpture you've chosen to be molded. Warm the clay in your hands and carefully and evenly press it around the doll's face. Gently pull off the clay. Place it on a baking sheet and bake twice as long as the manufacturer's directions indicate, but do not exceed the recommended temperature. Let cool.

3. Press clay into the face mold and trim off the excess. Remove the clay face.

4. To make the clay wings, press clay into an assortment of seashells, trim off the excess, and remove the clay shells.

5. Gently press the clay face and seashells onto the base.

6. Make several tiny clay balls and press them onto the base. Punch holes in all these balls.

7. Roll out thin ribbons of clay and roll them up into flower shapes; press them onto the base.

8. Punch a hole in the base for holding the ribbon hanger.

9. Place the base on the baking sheet and bake it according to manufacturer's directions.

10. Cut the mirror shape, sand the edges, and glue it in place.

11. Glue on fabric to cover the back

12. Slip a length of ribbon through the hole.

Sleeping Cherub

Wouldn't a drowsy little angel crawl into a leaf for a nap? Designer Dolly Lutz Morris thinks so and modeled this tiny cherub after her daughter, Margaret, who looks like an angel...when she's asleep.

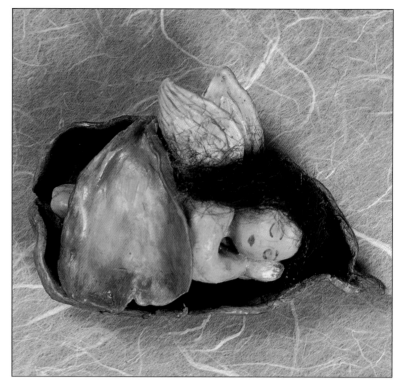

Designer: Dolly Lutz Morris

Size: 2 inches (5 cm)

Materials ▾

uncolored polymer clay

acrylic paints in colors of your choice

spray sealer

wool doll's hair

antiquing medium*

*brown stain mixed with paint thinner or
brown acrylic paint thinned with water makes
an excellent medium*

Tools ▾

oven or toaster oven

aluminum foil

metal nail file (or sharp clay tool)

paintbrushes

soft cloth

Instructions ▾

1. To make the leaf, make an oval measuring 1/8 x 1-1/2 x 3-1/4 inches (.5 x 4 x 8.5 cm). Curl up the edges of the leaf and make veins with the nail file. Bake the leaf on aluminum foil according to the manufacturer's directions. Cool.

2. To make the body, shape a torso from a clay oval measuring 3/4 x 1-1/2 inches (2 x 4 cm). Place the torso on the leaf and add the head, made from a 3/4-inch (2 cm) ball, to the torso top by blending the two pieces together with your fingers.

3. Form the legs from coils, each 1/4 x 1 inch (1 x 2.5 cm). Add the legs to the torso, curving them into a sleeping position. Add small balls of clay for the feet and blend the feet into the legs.

4. For the arms, make coils measuring 1/4 x 3/4 inch (1 x 2.5 cm) and taper them at one end for the hands. Join the arms to the body and blend. Draw fingers on the hands with a file.

5. Make the wings from 3/4 x 1-inch (2 x 2.5 cm) teardrop shapes. Join them onto the back of the torso and leaf. Draw feather shapes on the wings with the file.

6. For the petal blanket, make a very thin teardrop shape measuring 1-1/4 x 1-3/4 inches (3 x 4.5 cm) and curl up the edges of the clay like a rose petal.

7. Place the entire piece on foil and bake per manufacturer's instructions. Cool.

8. Paint with acrylic paints and allow it to dry.

9. Spray with sealer.

10. To give the finished piece an aged look, brush with antiquing medium, then wipe off the stain until you achieve the desired effect.

11. Glue on the wool hair.

Clay Flower Angel

Designer Dolly Lutz Morris combines her love of flowers with her fascination with angels in this delicate ornament that looks equally pretty on the Christmas tree or hanging in a sunny window.

Designer: Dolly Lutz Morris
Size: 5 inches (13 cm)

Materials ▾

self-hardening clay
1/4 x 6-inch (1 x 15.5 cm) ribbon
acrylic paints in colors of your choice
paper clip
spray sealer

Tools ▾

metal nail file (or similar sharp object)
paintbrushes

Instructions ▾

1. For the leaf wings, make four clay "teardrops," 1/8 x 1-1/2 x 2-1/2 inches (.5 x 4 x 6.5 cm) each. Curl the leaf edges and carve veins into the leaves with the file. Arrange the wings on a work surface with the top leaves pointing up and the bottom leaves pointing down.

2. To make the torso, place a clay oval, 1/4 x 1 x 1-1/4 inches (1 x 3 cm), onto the wings. Turn the piece over and blend the wings onto the torso with your fingers.

3. Make the head from a 3/4-inch (2 cm) oval, slightly pointed at the chin. Add the head to the back of the torso and blend in the same manner.

4. For the skirt, make six petals, each 1/8 x 1/2 x 3/4 inch (.5 x 1.5 x 2 cm), with points at one end. Attach the petals to the front of the torso, blending the clay together and overlapping the petals.

5. Make coils that measure 1/4 x 1/2 x 1-1/2 inches (1 x 1.5 x 4 cm) to use for the arms. Bend the coils in the middle for the elbows. Attach the arms to the shoulders and blend the pieces with your fingers. With the file, carve folds into the sleeves. Make a tiny clay ball and blend it into the sleeves to make the hands.

6. Add the hair, blending it into the head and over the wings, and texture it with the nail file.

7. Add the daisy petal halo around the head and blend.

8. Push the paper clip into the back of the head and secure it well by blending and covering the clip with clay.

9. Allow the piece to air-dry thoroughly.

10. Paint the entire piece with a white acrylic base coat and allow it to dry.

11. Paint over the base coat with acrylic washes, one part water to three parts paint.

12. Seal with spray sealer.

13. Attach the ribbon through the paper clip and tie.

Kneeling Angel

Dolly Lutz Morris often customizes her precious kneeling angels by placing flowers, birds, balls, dolls, or anything a child would hold into the angel's hands.

Designer: Dolly Lutz Morris
Size: 5 inches (13 cm)

Materials ▾

paper mache mix

acrylic paints in colors of your choice

spray sealer

antiquing medium*

posterboard

cellophane tape

paper or plastic plate

*brown stain thinned with paint thinner or brown acrylic paint thinned with water makes a good medium

Tools ▾

metal nail file

scissors

mixing bowl

paintbrushes

soft cloth

Instructions ▾

1. Construct a posterboard cone measuring 4-1/2 inches (11.5 cm) tall and 2 inches (5 cm) at the base. Tape the cone together to make the base of the angel body.

2. Cut a heart shape, 3-1/2 x 3-1/2 inches (9 x 9 cm), from the posterboard to form the angel's wings. Tape the wings to the back of the cone with the highest point on the wings even with the top of the cone.

3. Cover the wings and cone with a thickness of 1/4-inch (1 cm) paper mache and allow the angel to dry. Place the figure on a paper plate so you can turn the piece and view it from all sides while you work.

4. Make the head of a 1-inch (2.5 cm) ball of paper mache and attach it to the top of the cone. Do not add the hair yet.

5. Add some paper mache to the front bottom of the cone to suggest knees under the robe.

6. Build the paper mache form out from the back of the angel to resemble legs underneath a robe. The figure should measure about 3 inches (7.5 cm) from knees to heels. Add two 1/4-inch (1 cm) ovals to the ends of the legs for feet.

7. Add more paper mache to the front of the robe to form folds of draped fabric. Using a nail file, shape and texture the folds.

8. Make 1/2 x 1-1/2-inch (1.5 x 4 cm)

coils and bend them in the center to form the arms. Attach them to the shoulders and blend. Make the folds and details with the file.

9. Shape two 1/4-inch (1 cm) balls into oval-shaped praying hands and position them between the sleeves. Blend.

10. Make the hair by adding several thin layers of mache to the head, back, and shoulders, shaping and adding texture with the file.

11. Allow the figure to dry thoroughly, and then paint it with acrylic paints.

12. Spray the angel with sealer and let it dry.

13. Apply the antiquing medium and wipe off the excess medium with a cloth until you get the desired aged effect. Dry thoroughly.

14. Spray the final sealer coat.

▶ *Angels and ministers of grace defend us.*

WILLIAM SHAKESPEARE

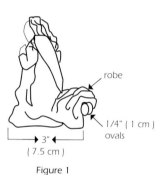

Figure 1

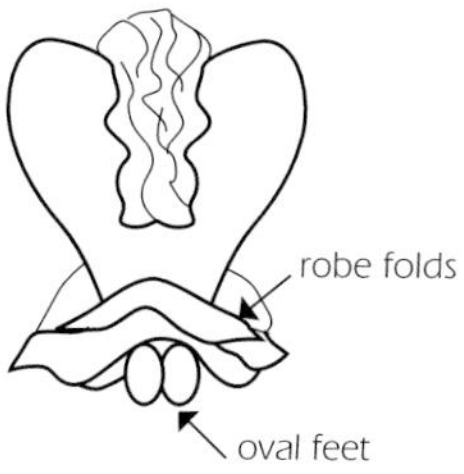

Figure 2

Designer: Dolly Lutz Morris
Size: 3 x 3 inches (7.5 x 7.5 cm)

Salt Dough Angels

Gold leaf paint adds an elegant touch to these ornaments designed by Dolly Lutz Morris and made from ever-popular salt dough.

Materials ▾

aluminum foil

salt dough (recipe below)

acrylic paints in white and colors of your choice

glitter paint

gold leaf paint

antiquing medium*

paper clips

spray sealer

gold cord

wool doll's hair

white glue

1/4-inch (1 cm) ribbon

*brown stain mixed with paint thinner or brown acrylic paint thinned with water makes an excellent medium

Tools ▾

metal nail file

pencil

paintbrushes

soft cloth scrap

Basic Salt Dough Recipe

    1 cup (240 ml) table salt

    1/2 cup (120 ml) cornstarch

    3/4 cup (180 ml) cold water

Mix the ingredients together in the top of a double boiler placed over medium heat. Stirring constantly, cook two or three minutes until the mixture thickens and begins to follow the spoon. Continue stirring over heat until the mixture is the consistency of bread dough. Remove from heat and let it cool. Turn mixture onto the counter and knead until smooth. The dough can be stored in a plastic bag for several days.

Traditional Ornament

1. Make 3 x 4 x 4-inch (7.5 x 10.5 x 10.5 cm) triangle for the angel robe. Note: all dough pieces should be about 1/4 inch (1 cm) thick. Using the file, make the robe and vest details. Make the skirt ruffles by pressing your fingers into the dough.

2. Form a head from a 3/4-inch (2 cm) ball. Attach it to the neck and blend. Push a paper clip into the back of the head for a hanger.

3. Add the hair and halo, blending both into the head and shoulders.

4. Make the wings, 2 x 3 inches (5 x 7.5 cm), and attach to the back and blend. Using the file, draw feathers on the wings.

5. Shape the dough into two triangles, then bend them slightly in the center to form the arms. Attach the arms to the shoulders, blend, and bring the arms together across the waist of the angel. Make the sleeve details with the file.

6. Allow the figure to air-dry as long as two days depending on the weather and humidity.

7. Apply a base coat of white acrylic paint and allow the angel to dry.

8. Paint the figure. Allow it to dry. Paint the gold details and let that dry.

9. Spray the angel with sealer. Dry. Apply the antiquing medium, and wipe off with a soft cloth until you achieve the desired aged effect. Spray with the sealer.

10. Attach the gold cord to the paper clip and tie.

Angel in Blue Apron

Instructions are essentially the same as for the Traditional Ornament except:

1. The skirt is crimped by lifting the edges with a pencil point.

2. The apron is added to the top of the skirt and the edges are also crimped.

3. Add detail to the wings with a file, using long strokes.

4. Add tiny, flattened ball cheeks to the angel's face.

5. Attach the hair as a final step, after the figure is dry.

Note: Dough ornaments will keep for many years if they are sprayed all over with sealer (to keep out moisture) and stored in a dry place.

Designer: Dolly Lutz Morris
Size: 4-1/2 x 6 inches (11.5 x 15.5 cm)

Paper Angel Ornaments

Designed by Dolly Lutz Morris, these joyful angels look like expensive paper ornaments from the Victorian Age. But with these simple materials, you can afford to trim the whole tree!

Materials ▾

tracing paper
3/4-inch (2 cm) brass star
posterboard
fine-line black permanent marker
acrylic paints in colors of your choice
glitter paint
glitter stars
gold thread
spray sealer
white glue

Tools ▾

scissors
handsewing needle
paintbrushes

Instructions ▾

1. Trace the angels onto good quality tracing paper, not tissue. Spray the tracings with sealer so they won't run or bleed, and allow the pattern to dry.

2. Apply glue to the back of the tracings and affix the angels to a piece of posterboard.

3. Cut out the angels.

4. Paint the angels with the acrylics, using the photograph as your guide. Touch up the black lines with permanent marker, if needed. Spray the angels with sealer and allow to dry.

5. Brush on the glitter paint and glue on the stars.

6. With gold thread, sew the brass star to the angel's hand.

7. With gold thread, sew on hangers.

Enlarge all 133%

Book of Angels

For special dinners, designer Mary Jane Miller scatters her dining table with candles and these delightful "flights of angels." These angel books also make wonderful greeting cards or gifts.

Designer: Mary Jane Miller
Size: 3 x 21 inches (7.5 x 54 cm)

Materials ▾

decorative paper (marbled, wallpaper, construction)

white glue

(2) 3 x 3 inch (7.5 x 7.5 cm) squares cardboard or matboard

9 inches (23 cm) of 1/8-inch (.5 cm) ribbon

paints (watercolors or acrylics) in colors of your choice

gold or silver markers or paint

felt tip markers or crayons

Tools ▾

scissors

paintbrushes

Instructions ▾

1. Cut the decorative paper into 3-inch (7.5 cm) strips at least 21 inches (54 cm) long.

2. Fold the strips back and forth accordion-style until you have a 3-inch (7.5 cm) square.

3. Trim the edges with scissors if necessary.

4. Trace the angel pattern onto the paper square and cut out the pattern as you cut paper dolls, being careful to keep the folds joined at the hands and feet.

5. Paint or decorate the "chain" of angels and set it aside.

6. Cut two identical pieces of cardboard or matboard, 3 x 3 inches (7.5 x 7.5 cm) each, or to fit over the folded angels.

7. Glue decorative paper on one side of each piece of board.

8. Glue the first angel on the back of the top book cover; glue the last angel on the inside of the back cover.

9. Decorate the inside of the book covers as you like, perhaps with gold or silver pens or paint.

10. Secure the ribbon onto the center of the back book cover with glue or a handmade sticker (shown here) made of a paper scrap and glue.

Paper Twist Angels

Paper twist angels are a simple and traditional folk craft. These sweet ones, made by Lesa Winchester, will add a homey touch to your Christmas tree.

Designer: Lesa Winchester

Sizes: 4-1/2 inches (11.5 cm) and 6 inches (15.5 cm)

Mauve and Tan Angel

14 inches (36 cm) paper twist in color of your choice

9 inches (23 cm) tan or ivory paper twist

1-inch (2.5 cm) wooden ball (predrilled) with 1/2 (1.5 cm) hole

narrow gold cord

gold-look wedding band

hot glue

Red Angel

(2) 9-inch (23 cm) paper twists in color of your choice

1/2-inch (1.5 cm) wooden ball with pre-painted face

narrow gold cord

gold-look wedding band

hot glue

Tools ▾

glue gun

scissors

Mauve and Tan Angel

1. From the 14-inch (36 cm) piece, cut 5-1/2 (14 cm) inches of colored paper twist to use for the arms and untwist it.

2. Fold the remaining 8-1/2-inch (22 cm) piece in half and insert the two cut ends into the holes in the wooden ball. Pull 2 inches (5 cm) of paper out of the top of the ball and fold it around the ball to make a hood.

3. Slip the arm section between the folded paper under the head. Twist the hand end so that the arms look gathered.

4. Use the gold cord or ribbon to tie under the arms and around the back (in an x-shape) to secure the arms.

5. Open flat the 9-inch (23 cm) section of tan or ivory paper twist. To make the wings, fold in one end of the paper to the center, and then fold the other end in until it overlaps the other cut end. Slightly gather the center of the paper to make a bow shape and glue the bow together. Glue the bow to the back of the angel below the neck. Make a hanger from a loop of gold cord and glue on.

6. For a halo, glue on the gold band.

Red Angel

1. Untwist the two pieces of paper twist.

2. Fold one piece in half and tie gold cord around it about a 1/2 inch (1.5 cm) down to make a collar.

3. With the other piece of paper twist, follow step 5 above to make the wings.

4. Glue on the wooden face and the gold band for a halo.

Tarjeteria Mistletoe Angel

Tarjeteria is the Puerto Rican art of creating embossed paper items for greeting cards, bookmarks, gift tags, or shaped paper projects such as this delicate, translucent angel, designed by Susan Dilán.

▶ *In this dim world of clouding cares, We rarely know, till 'wildered eyes See white wings lessening up the skies, The angels with us unawares.*

GERALD MASSEY

Designer: Susan R. Dilán
Size: 6 inches (15 cm)

Materials ▾

8-1/2 x 11-inch (22 x 28 cm) piece of
   Tarjeteria paper (heavy tracing vellum)*

#00 technical pen with black ink

colored pencils: white, red, green, yellow,
   brown, and light brown

1/8 x 6-inches (.5 x 15 cm) light blue ribbon

removable transparent tape

wide-tipped gold paint marker (optional)

Tools ▾

small ball-tipped burnisher tool with
   rubber pad

Calado tool set or single needle stylus
   tool*

scissors: 1 pair straight edge and 1 pair
   fine-point embroidery

*Artemus & Co., 30-22 10 St., Villa Carolina,
   Carolina, PR 00985, (809) 768-6535.*

Instructions ▾

1. Place the Tarjeteria paper over the pattern and tape in place. Use the white colored pencil to trace around the skirt of the angel and the wings. Use the black technical pen to trace the angel's face, body, and mistletoe. Do not trace any of the lace design (called the Calado work) on the skirt or around the edge of the wings.

2. To do the Calado work, place the paper and pattern on a firm rubber pad. Use the #4 (4 needles which form a square) and the #4L (4 needles in a line) Calado tools to pierce the design where indicated. Carefully remove the angel from the pattern and place it on the rubber pad so the design faces down. Use the small ball burnisher to add the dots and to draw around the Calado design, and to draw the lines on the angel's wings.

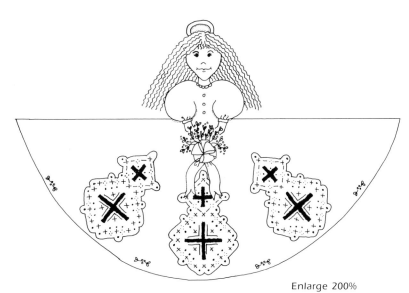

Enlarge 200%

KEY TO CHART

∷ = pierced with #4 Calado tool

X = pierced with #4 Calado tool, then cut

⋯⋯ = pierced with #4L Calado tool

• = burnished

▬ = pierced in continuous line with #4
   Cadado tool (∷∷∷) then cut out (=∶=∶)
   and center removed to form opening

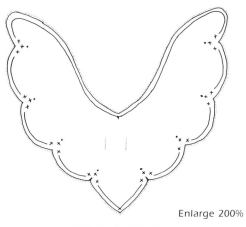

Enlarge 200%

KEY TO CHART

+ = pierced with #4 Calado tool,
   then cut to form x

• = burnished

⋯⋯ = pierced with #4L Calado tool

Note: In Tarjeteria, burnishing creates both highlights and embossing at the same time. Burnishing is done by placing the paper on a firm rubber pad and pushing on the paper with a ball-tipped burnishing tool. There are two basic strokes: drawing and highlighting. To draw, the burnisher is used like a pencil, firmly tracing the indicated area. To highlight, the burnisher is used like a paintbrush, raising the burnisher at the end of each stroke.

3. To add the cutwork to the Calado, remove the angel from the pattern. To form the small x's, insert the fine-point scissors into the adjacent hole of #4 pierces and snip as if cutting the four sides of a small square. To create the large open x designs, pierce along the wide black lines with the #4 Calado tool, cut completely around the design with the fine-point scissors, and remove the excess paper from the center of the design.

4. On the back side of the angel, color the ribbon red, the hair brown, and the face light brown. On the front side, color the mistletoe leaves green, and the buttons and halo yellow; lightly color the angel's lips and cheeks red.

5. To emboss, place the angel, design side down, on the rubber pad. Use the small ball burnisher to completely burnish the mistletoe leaves and berries, the buttons, the collar and cuff of the angel's blouse, her bottom lip, and her halo. Also draw along the lines of her hair, and create a linen look by very lightly stroking a woven (crisscross) pattern on her blouse. To add dimension to the bow on her skirt, use a highlighting stroke on the tips of the ribbon toward the bow and on each section of the bow from the outside edge toward the center. To add extra depth, turn the design over and completely burnish the inner portion of each bow section.

6. To assemble the angel, use the #4L Calado tool to pierce the perforated lines where indicated on the wings, inside the halo (remove excess paper), and under the arms on both sides. Use the straight-edge scissors to cut out the angel. Slightly overlap the corners of the skirt in the back and tape underneath to hold. Run the thin ribbon through the perforations under the angel's arms and through the wings, then tie a bow in the back. To help hold the wings in place, insert the slots on the wings into the angel's skirt in the back.

Designer: Claudia Lee
Size: 4 x 7 inches (10 x 18 cm)

Green-Winged Angel

This spirited angel, designed by Claudia Lee, seems eager to bring joy and peace to some lucky mortal.

Except for the design, this project is identical to the one on page 120.

Cut Paper Garlands

Designed by Marie-Helene Grabman, these simple angels look wonderful ringing a Christmas tree or propped on a mantel or sunny windowsill.

Designer: Marie-Helene Grabman
Size: 4 x 6 inches (10.5 x 15.5 cm) per angel

Materials ▾
medium-weight paper

Tools ▾
scissors
craft knife
pencil

Instructions ▾

1. Copy the design from the book onto scratch paper and cut out the pattern. Cut out both the overall shape and the interior spaces.

2. Accordion-fold a piece of paper. The number of layers of paper you end up with will be the number of angels in your garland. Make sure the folded paper is as wide as you want the images to be.

3. Trace the pattern onto the folded paper.

4. Cut out the figure, being careful not to cut through the dotted lines on either side of the figure. Use the craft knife to cut out the small interior designs.

5. Unfold the paper to admire your garland.

Collage Angel Magnets

Elegant and so simple to make, these angel magnets are the creation of Mary Jane Miller. Here the artist uses marbled paper designed by Mimi Schleicher.

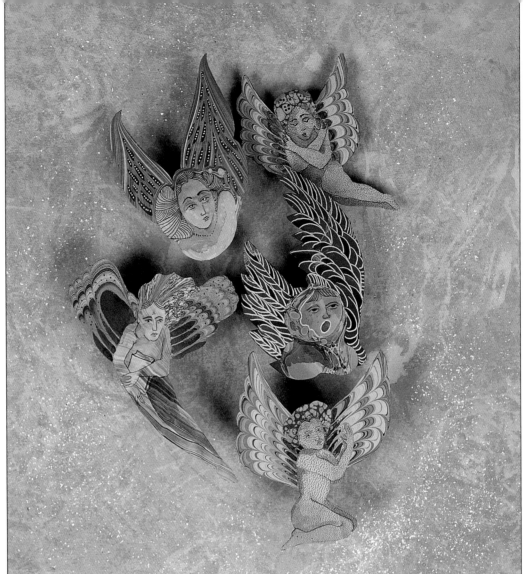

Designer: Mary Jane Miller
Size: 2-1/2 x 3 inches (6.5 x 7.5 cm)

Materials ▾

decorative paper (marbled, wallpaper, wrap, construction, tissue)

sheets of magnetic rubber (from craft store)

acrylic or watercolor paints in colors of your choice

felt tip pens

gold or silver paint pens

white glue

clear spray enamel

Tools ▾

scissors

paintbrushes

Instructions ▾

1. Using a favorite angel image from a drawing, picture, greeting card, or this book, trace the image onto the paper, or compose your own angel image. Use different papers for the wings, face, body, and hair.

2. Assemble the paper collage directly onto the magnetic rubber sheet, being careful to use the nonmagnetic side.

3. Glue the collage into place, layering when necessary, and allow glue to dry thoroughly.

4. Cut out the angel with scissors.

5. Highlight and embellish the angel with ink, felt tip markers, paint, or gold and silver paint pens. Here's your chance to be creative.

6. To finish, spray with a clear enamel.

Note: Don't need a refrigerator magnet? Use this same technique on nice paper to create greeting cards or art suitable for framing.

► *Oh sovereign angel,*

Wide winged Stranger above a forgetful earth,

Care for me, care for me. Keep me unaware of danger

And not regretful

And not forgetful of my innocent birth..

EDNA ST. VINCENT MILLAY

Angel Wings

Slip into something heavenly with these exquisite adult-size wings designed by Suzanne Koppi. You'll look and feel like an angel (batteries for flying are not included).

Materials ▾

4 yards (4 m) 60-inch-wide (154 cm) fabric for wing "skin"

4 yards (4 m) 60-inch-wide (154 cm) fabric for lining

1 yard (92.5 cm) lace material for feathers (shimmery)

1-3/4 yards (1.75 m) of 36-inch-wide (92.5 cm) foam sheeting 1-inch-thick (2.5 cm)

2 metal clothes hangers

matching thread

fabric crafts adhesive

24 x 36 inches (61.5 x 92.5 cm) batting scraps (approximate)

newspaper (3 or 4 sheets)

Tools ▾

hand sewing and sewing machine equipment

wire cutters

Instructions ▾

1. Using the pattern, cut a pair of wings from the foam. If possible, try to cut it in one piece; if any piecing is required, use a small amount of fabric adhesive. Trim the corner edges of the wings to give them roundness.

2. Using the same pattern, but adding 1-1/2 inches (4 cm) to the top edges and 1 inch (2.5 cm) to the bottom edges for ease, and 2 inches (5 cm) to the center lines for seam allowances, cut four pieces of the "skin" fabric and four pieces of the lining fabric—all cut on the bias.

3. Straighten out the coat hangers. Cut off the hooks and coil segments of each. Bend the wire to match the placement of the lines on the pattern. Lay the wire on top of the foam according to this placement and use glue to secure. Cut strips of batting 1-1/2 inches (4 cm) wide to cover the length of the wire and lay them on top of the wire; glue in place.

4. Cut two pieces of batting about 13 inches (33.5 cm) wide and the length of the top of each wing. For each wing: Fold under 2-1/2 - 3 inches (6.6 - 7.5 cm) of batting along the long side and place along the top of the side with wire (forming what will be a thickened area representing muscle along the shoulder of the wing); lap the remaining 5 inches (13 cm) across the top and down the back of the top. Shape with your fingers along the edge as it approaches the tip of the wing, trimming if necessary. Glue or hand stitch in place.

5. Using the lining fabric, stitch the right sides of each wing together in 1/2-inch (1.5 cm) seams, clip the curves, turn, and press lightly. Stitch the center seam of the lining only on one side; i.e., from one seam to the other. Finger-press open.

6. Gently feed the wings into the lining one at a time with the opening toward the side with the wire and the thicker muscle mass.

Make sure the wing tips fit into the corners and curves of the lining. Lap the opening edges and glue or hand stitch together securely (they will not show). Set this aside.

7. Prepare the skin fabric in the same manner as the lining in step 5.

8. Cut the feathers on the bias from the remnants of the skin fabric and the lace. You will need about 600 feathers, about one-tenth from lace.

9. Place a layer of newspaper inside the wing skin to protect it from excess glue. Place the skin on a clean tabletop with the opening down. Visualize how the feathers will lie on the wing before you begin to glue. Start with the bottom edge, place and glue a row of feathers. Use mostly the skin fabric; at varying intervals place a lace feather, usually about every 5-7 spaces. As you begin the second row, overlap the feathers by about 1-1/2 inches (4 cm) or whatever looks pleasing to you. Continue until the entire wing is covered, curving to account for the shape of the wing as you go. As you reach the top leave the last 1/2 inch (1.5 cm) or so uncovered. Along the top edge of the wing you will make a triple row of feathers beginning at the wing tip and working back to the shoulder. The trio of feathers

in each group will be placed similar to a fleur de lis with the two side feathers placed first and the center feather on top. *Optional:* When the glue has dried on this side, you may cover the inside of the wing with feathers, or cover the inside with a very soft short-pile fur.

10. When the feathers are dry, gently feed the wing into the skin. The wire side goes toward the unfeathered side. Do not join the opening edges yet.

11. Decide what garment you will be using for supporting your wings. (The project pictured here used a cream color, linen vest.)

From skin fabric, cut two rectangles measured to match the area between the actual wings plus 1/2-inch (1.5 cm) seam allowances. Stitch the rectangles with right sides together, turn, press, and close. Put on the garment and decide on the wing placement. Have someone mark the top, bottom, and center. Remove the garment and place the rectangle according to the marks, top stitching close to the top and bottom edges. Do not allow for the fullness of the wing, as you want it to fit very snugly to the garment.

12. Very gently feed the wings through the opening behind the rectangle and adjust the wrinkles and bulges that will result. Put the garment on and note whether the wings hold their own weight to your satisfaction. If not, you may wish to insert and secure a length of wire inside the wing behind your shoulders for added support. Please note that if you do this you will not be able to go through doorways (a pleasing feature of this design!). If you are happy with the arrangement, you may choose to remove the wings and close the last opening.

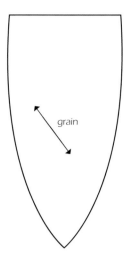

Feather pattern

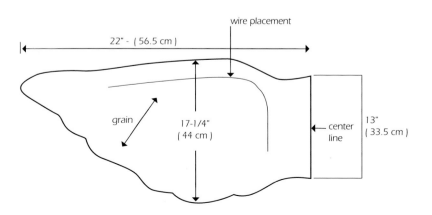

Designers: Lula Chang, Cathi Rosengren
Size: 6 x 8 inches (15.5 x 20.5 cm)

Needlepoint Angel: Canvas and Handbag

The angels that designer Lula Chang paints on canvas are extraordinarily expressive, and the quality of her color selection is very high: she meticulously hand paints every chart herself. Expert needlepointer Cathi Rosengren designed the stitch guide, completed the needlepoint, and turned the piece into a handbag. The result is truly heavenly.

Materials ▾

2 skeins Frosty Rays Y72
1 skein Cresta d'Oro C53, C48, C04
    (optional C10)
1 skein Flair F572, F575, F502
1 skein Watercolors Emerald
1 skein Medici Noir
1 skein Anchor floss 403, 778, 868

Tools ▾

tapestry needles
scissors

Instructions ▾

1. *Angel's face and hands:* Basketweave as painted, using floss 6-ply (or 3-ply doubled). For the eyes and mouth, do cross-stitch as painted, using floss 4-ply (2-ply doubled).

2. *Tree:* Use Watercolors Emerald 2-ply (or use 1-ply doubled). Basketweave tree. With Cresta d'Oro C04, basketweave or do continental stitches for touches of gold. Break this fiber; do not cut!

3. *Dress:* With Frosty Rays Y72 (cut this fiber on a severe diagonal) on the left side, do a diagonal mosaic variation coming from the wings toward the tree. When you have completed your downward row, return up the row, filling in a continental or basketweave stitch to meet every other short stitch. Thread another needle with Cresta d'Oro C04 and fill in the skipped upward stitches with a French knot. Pull your needle with gold to a holding position and complete your next downward row in diagonal mosaic stitch. For the right side, you will turn the work so it is slanting in the appropriate direction from the wing to the tree.

4. *Neck band and cuffs of dress:* Use Cresta d'Oro C53 and C48 as painted, using alternating Smyrna stitches. Remember to break this fiber—do not cut!

5. *Wings:* With Flair F502 and F575 as painted, execute the interlocking Gobelin stitch over three horizonal threads. Cut this fiber on a severe diagonal. Tack it back through the needle so that the needle does not fall out.

6. *Wreath:* Using Watercolors Emerald, basketweave all the leaves. With Frosty Rays Y72, complete French knots for the holly berries. Using Cresta d'Oro C04, do Smyrna stitches for the gold highlights.

7. *Halo:* Using Flair F572, cover the painted area with long Gobelin stitches in one direction; then return and do them in the opposite direction. This will add a beautiful padded effect to the halo.

8. *Hair:* Using Medici Noir 4-ply (or 2-ply doubled), do loose French knots. Wrap your knot only once, but don't wrap it tightly. The easiest way to do these is to continue in a basketweave fashion.

9. Finish the angel by stitching two or three "garbage rows" around the angel in a color of your choice so she can easily be finished as an ornament.

10. *Handbag variation:* Using Medici Noir execute a Scotch stitch over three, turning each stitch to face each other. When finished, backstitch between stitches, using Cresta d'Oro C10.

Note: All these stitches appear in needlepoint books. Trace the photo to create your pattern.

Cherub Sweater

Designer Nola Theiss used duplicate stitch and twin cherubs to impart an angelic air to a premade baby sweater.

Designer: Nola Theiss
Gauge: 28 sts x 36 rows
Size of motif: 31 sts x 28 rows

Materials ▾

premade baby sweater (or knit your own)

yarn that matches the weight of the sweater: gold, yellow, blue, and peach

heart motif or other decorative button

sewing thread

Tools ▾

embroidery needle

sewing needle

Instructions ▾

1. Center the chart on the front with the cherubs facing each other and use duplicate stitch to create the design.

2. Use an outline stitch to embroider the eye in blue.

3. Sew on the heart or decorative button as shown in the photograph.

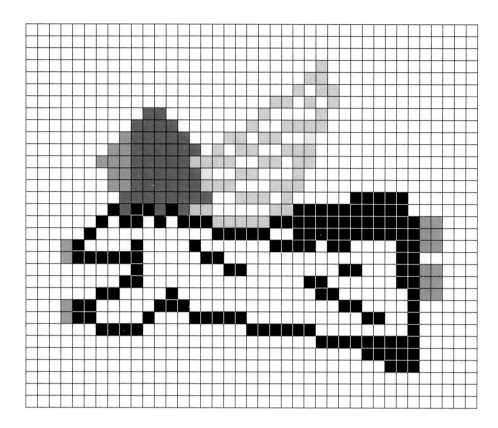

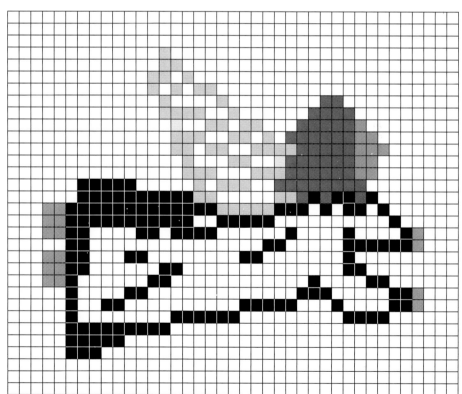

KEY TO CHART

dark gray = gold

light gray = yellow

black = blue

medium gray = peach

Angel Pin

Dolly Lutz Morris, creator of this enchanting pin, recommends using uncolored clay and paint instead of colored clay. This method gives the pin a more ancient, timeless look.

Designer: Dolly Lutz Morris
Size: 1-1/2 x 1-3/4 inches (4 x 4.5 cm)

Materials ▾

aluminum foil

1-inch pin back fitting

uncolored polymer clay

antiquing medium*

acrylic paints in colors of your choice

white glue

spray sealer

brown stain mixed with paint thinner or brown acrylic paint thinned with water makes an excellent medium

Tools ▾

oven or toaster oven

metal nail file or sculpting tool

paintbrushes

soft cloth scrap

Instructions ▾

1. Make a clay oval measuring 1/4 x 1-1/2 x 1-3/4 inches (1 x 4 x 4.5 cm). Bake the oval on foil as per manufacturer's directions and cool.

2. To make the angel robe, add a 1/8-inch (.5 cm) layer of the clay to the base and sculpt with a file to create the folds and details.

3. In the same manner, make the sleeves and attach them to the robe, blending the pieces together with your fingers.

4. Add a 1/8-inch (.5 cm) ball for the head; then add the hair. Carve details into the pieces with the nail file.

5. Add the wings and create the feather effect by drawing on the wings with the file.

6. Bake, cool, and paint.

7. Spray with sealer.

8. Apply the antiquing medium and wipe medium off with the soft cloth until you achieve the desired aged effect. Let the piece dry.

9. Spray the angel with sealer two or three times, drying between coats.

10. Glue on the pin fitting.

Sweetheart T-Shirt

Ellen Zahorec designed this adorable T-shirt with simple and appealing shapes, including wings made with a ring of hearts.

Designer: Ellen Zahorec

Materials ▾

100% cotton T-shirt

acrylic fabric paints: pink, purple, yellow, gold, flesh, red, blue, and gold glitter

stencil set with alphabet and shapes

fine-tipped indelible black marker

Tools ▾

cellulose painting sponges

Instructions ▾

1. With the black marker, draw the angel using the photograph as a guide.

2. Use the stencil set and sponge on the hearts, stars, and letters.

3. Add black lines for detail.

4. Sponge on the gold glitter to accent the stars, hands, and halo.

Guardian Angel Pin

This charming pin was inspired by a 30 foot hallway mural painted by designer Jacqueline Janes' stepmother in which 14 angels frolic in the sky. This piece clearly demonstrates that big ideas can take flight on very small wings.

Designer: Jacqueline Janes
Size: 1-3/4 inches (4.5 cm)

▶ *Everyone, no matter how humble he may be, has angels to watch over him. They are heavenly pure and splendid, and yet they have been given us to keep us company on our way.*

POPE PIUS XII

Materials ▾

polymer clay:

1 block white

1/2 block grey

1/4 block pink

1/8 block rosewood

1/8 block champagne

small piece caramel

small piece yellow

premade or purchased face (16 mm)

premade flower cane

scraps of two or three other colors

10 eye pins

pin back

Tools ▾

craft knife

slicing blade

wire cutters

Instructions ▾

1. Begin with the angel's body. Flatten a piece of white clay into a rectangle 1/4 inch (1 cm) thick. With a craft knife, make four cuts in the rectangle (figure 1). Flatten a piece of grey clay 1/4 inch (1 cm) thick and cut four very thin strips. Pull apart the cuts in the rectangle and insert the grey strips. Reshape the rectangle and close any gaps by pinching together. With the slicing blade, shave 1/16 inch (.25 cm) off the front of the rectangle. Shape the bottom of the rectangle into a skirt.

2. To make the sash, create a striped loaf using the pink and rosewood. Cut a thin slice of the loaf and wrap it around the body. Secure the sash by pressing together where it meets on the hip.

3. To make the collar, depress the top of the body in the center with your thumb (this creates the neckline). Cut very thin slices of the flower cane and place it around the neckline.

4. Press the corners of the rectangle gently with your fingers to create shoulders.

5. For the arms, make two small rectangles with the white clay cut 1/4 inch (1 cm) thick. Make another striped loaf with the pink and rosewood and cut a 1/4-inch-thick (1 cm) piece from the loaf. Cut apart the white rectangle and place the striped loaf piece in between the two (figure 2). Repeat with the other rectangle. Round the

top outside corners of the rectangle to finish the shoulders.

6. To make the hands, create a striped loaf with the brown (five sheets) and champagne (six sheets). Flip the loaf so the stripes are facing downward and place a 1/4-inch-thick (1 cm) sheet on top of the loaf. Cut a 1/4-inch-thick (1 cm) slice of the loaf and press it into the bottom of the arm. Repeat with the other arm.

7. To make the shoes, flatten a piece of yellow clay into a 3/4-inch-thick (2 cm) rectangle. Use the craft knife to cut the rectangle into the shape shown in figure 3. Cut two 1/4-inch (1 cm) pieces and place a small slice of flower cane on each shoe.

8. For the wings, flatten the scrap clay into a rectangle 1/8 inch (.5 cm) thick. Cut in half and place one piece on top of the other. Use the craft knife to cut out the shape of the wing (figure 4). Separate the two pieces and press together at the small, squared end. To make a feather cane, first fashion a rectangular loaf with the white clay and make four cuts at a 45-degree angle. Flatten the grey clay to 1/16 inch (.25 cm) thick and cut four strips. Insert the grey strips between the cuts in the white loaf and reassemble. Reduce the cane and cut in half. Place another thin strip of grey along one side of one of the pieces and press the two pieces together. Cut thin pieces of the cane and press them onto the wing shape, starting at the bottom. Overlap the pieces a little to create texture. Cover the entire surface of the wing shape.

9. With wire cutters, trim the eye pins to 1/4 inch (1 cm). Pair up the eye pins and join them together. Push the pins into all the pieces and then into the body.

10. Press the squared ends of the wings into the back of the body. Apply pressure to the middle of the back and gently pull the wings away from the body.

10. Bake all the pieces with the pins at 265 degrees for 30-40 minutes.

12. After all the pieces have cooled, remove the pins and glue them back in place. Add the head and glue the bottom of the head onto the shoulders. Apply a generous amount of glue to the base of the wings and glue the pin back to the back of the wings.

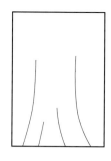

Figure 1

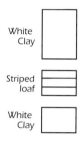

White Clay

Striped loaf

White Clay

Figure 2

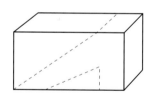

Figure 3

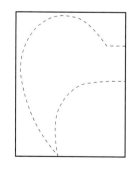

Figure 4

Designer: Mary S. Parker

Guardian Angel Applique Vest

With her wild hair and dazzling wings, the angel Mary Parker created for this vest looks celestial and sensational.

Materials ▾

vest pattern of your choice

enough fashion fabric to cut out 2 vest
fronts and 1 vest back

Enough lining fabric to cut out same

1 spool matching sewing thread

3/8 yard (34.5 cm) solid silver-colored
fabric

1 spool silver metallic thread

1/4 yard (23 cm) brocade for angel's dress

1 spool matching rayon or metallic thread

enough fusible tricot interfacing to make 2
vest fronts and 1 vest back

1 spool silver ribbon floss for angel's hair

1 spool invisible nylon thread

buttons for vest

Tools ▾

sewing machine

Instructions ▾

1. Prepare vest pattern as you normally
would. Cut out two vest fronts and one
vest back of: 1) fashion fabric, 2) lining
fabric, and 3) fusible interfacing.

2. Fuse the interfacing to wrong side of
the two vest fronts and the vest back.

3. From the silver fabric cut out: 2) the
wings, 2) hands, and 3) halo/neck/face
pieces. Be sure to include extensions indicated by dotted lines on the template.

4. From the brocade cut out the dress.

5. Position the wings where desired on
the vest front and/or vest back. Pin in
place and baste around all the edges.
Starting in the center of the wings, use
either a straight stitch or a decorative stitch
to create a vertical, curving line to suggest
the appearance of feathers. Stitch additional lines parallel to the first one, gradually
working on either side of the center out
toward the edges of the wings. Loosen the
basting stitch as you approach the edges of
the wings if the fabric has stretched as a
result of your stitching on it. When you
have covered the entire surface area of the
wings, satin stitch all around the perimeter.

6. Pin the dress in place on top of the
wings. Slide in the halo/face/neck piece
under the dress neck. Slide in the hand
pieces under the dress sleeves. When you
are satisfied with the relative positioning of
all pieces, baste around the perimeter of
the dress only. Do not baste around the
halo/face/neck piece or hand pieces yet.

7. Lift up the halo/face/neck piece slightly,
and mark on the fashion fabric where the
angel's chin will be when the piece is
appliquéd in place. Also mark the
position of the bottom of the halo
on the fashion fabric. These two
marks will be about 3/4 inch
(2 cm) apart.

8. So that it will be out of the
way while you create the
angel's hair design, fold down
the halo/face/neck piece back
over the dress and secure it
with one pin through the top
of the halo. Zigzag over the
individual strands of ribbon
floss with invisible nylon
thread to create the angel's
hair. Make wide arcs at the outer edges
of the design, but bring the strands
closer together as you reach the
center of the design so that all the
strands fit within the 3/4-inch
(2 cm) area.

9. When you are satisfied with the
amount of hair, fold the halo/face/neck
piece back in place. Pin and baste the
oval forming the angel's face. Then pin
and baste the halo, starting at the left
side of the face, going around the
perimeter of the halo, and ending at
the right side of the angel's face.
Finally, baste the neck, removing the
basting stitch on the dress if necessary to allow more or less of the
neck to extend out from under the
dress neck edge. Baste the neck of
the dress again.

10. Apply a few final strands of ribbon floss around the angel's face and
over the forehead to further define the
angel's face.

11. Satin stitch around the perimeter of
the halo from the ribbon floss hair on
one side to the ribbon floss hair on
the other side. Use a decorative stitch
to fill in the halo's interior to resemble stars.

12. Satin stitch the angel's neck from
where the ribbon floss hair ends on each
side down to the dress.

13. Straight stitch around the angel's hands.
You can satin stitch over this if desired.

14. Satin stitch around the angel's dress.

15. Construct the vest according to the
instructions given with the purchased
pattern.

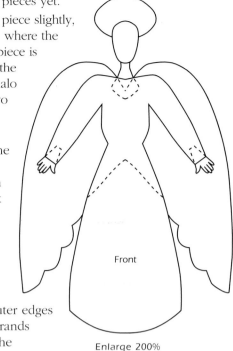

Front

Enlarge 200%

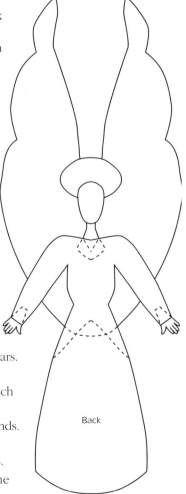

Back

Enlarge 200%

Designer: Carol Wilcox Wells
Size: 4 x 4-1/2 inches (10.5 x 11.5 cm)

Bead Embroidery Necklace

The halo on this magnificent angel (pearls and all) looks like a crown. Designed by Carol Wilcox Wells, the necklace is certain to impart regality to the lucky person who wears it.

Materials ▾

size 15 Japanese round seed beads in the following colors:

- silver lined clear
- transparent gold aurora borealis
- white opaque luster
- mauve opaque luster
- rich cream luster
- metallic copper
- metallic bronze
- lined teal
- metallic black violet
- purple gold luster

6 natural pink freshwater pearls

6 white freshwater pearls

6 x 6 inches (1.5 x 1.5 cm) cream silk bridal satin

ivory opaque knee hose

cream synthetic suede

DMC floss ecru and #315

20-inch (51 cm) gold chain

3 pieces of boning: (1) 3 inches (7.5 cm) long, (2) 2-1/2 inches (6.5 cm) long

polyester fiberfill

embroidery hoop

thread

Tools ▾

#12 beading needle

hand sewing needle

scissors

Instructions ▾

1. Transfer the drawing to the silk bridal satin and place the fabric on the embroidery hoop.

2. Cut a 3 x 3-inch (7.5 x 7.5 cm) piece from the knee hose. Stretch it lightly over the drawing and sketch the oval face. Cut around the oval 1/8 inch (.5 cm) larger than the drawing. Baste along the drawn oval.

3. Turn the raw edges of the hose under and sew it in place over the oval on the satin, leaving a small opening. Stuff with fiberfill and sew the opening closed.

4. Sew the halo pearls into place.

5. Using a backstitch technique, start embroidering the beads in place (figure 1). Pick up three to four beads, push them down to the end of the thread. Line the needle up with the other beads, push it through the fabric, come back up through the fabric one bead from the end, and go back through the remaining two to three beads. Pick up three to four beads and continue.

6. Do the halo first, then the wings, body, hair, and face.

7. Create the eyes and eyebrows with beads.

8. Stitch the nose with ecru floss to give it a three-dimensional effect. The lips are embroidered with #315 floss.

9. When you are finished embroidering the beads, take the fabric from the hoop and cut it 1/4 inch (1 cm) from the beaded design. Fold this edge under and baste it in place. Lay this on the synthetic suede and draw around the edge with pencil, being careful not to get graphite on the satin. Cut out the suede to fit the back of the bead embroidery.

10. Before attaching the suede, sew the boning in place. The boning material will be curved to give the angel a dimensional shape. Place the curved side of the boning to the back side of the bead embroidery (figure 2). Now carefully stitch on the suede backing.

11. Cut the gold chain in half (remove the cut links) and stitch the chain to the wings.

▸ *The soul at its highest is found like God, but an angel gives a closer idea of Him. That is all an angel is: an idea of God.*

MEISTER ECKHART

Figure 1

Figure 2

Designer: Susan Kinney

Size: Necklace size varies;
earrings are 2 inches (5 cm) long

Flying Cherub Necklace and Earrings

Designer Susan Kinney creates this eye-catching jewelry by first making cherub and angel beads from a mold. A gold wax finish transforms the clay into striking jewels.

Materials ▾

small metal cherub shape (found in craft stores)

1 block of black polymer clay

scrap polymer clay to make the cherub mold

gold buffing wax

2 feet (62 cm) black waxed linen cord

earring posts and backs

4 gold-tone head pins

glass beads (small black, medium black, and garnet)

flat gold spacer beads

spray sealer, matte finish

instant glue

Tools ▾

oven or toaster oven

needle nose pliers

wire clippers or strong scissors

clay-cutting blade

needle or piercing tool

Necklace

1. Roll out a ball of any color clay and press it onto the small metal cherub. Following the manufacturer's directions, bake the mold. When the clay is cool, remove the metal cherub. You now have your clay mold.

2. Press small balls of black clay into the mold and trim the excess with your blade. Carefully remove the cherub from the mold and, using your piercing tool or a needle, make a hole down through the head. Make eight cherubs.

3. For the center necklace cherub, you will need to mold two cherubs together, back to back. Pierce holes that go from the wings down through the cheeks and out through the chin.

4. To make the angel face beads, press pea-sized balls of black clay into the head portion of the mold. Remove carefully and pierce vertically with your tool. Make eight.

5. Place the cherubs and angel beads on a baking sheet and bake according to the manufacturer's directions. Cool, and buff with gold buffing wax. Spray the beads with a matte finish sealer.

6. Now for the threading. Begin at the center of the necklace with the three-dimensional cherub. Notice in the photograph that the linen cord has been knotted below the center cherub. Atop the knot is a small flat gold bead. From that point the cord is threaded through the cherub head and divided, with one strand going left and one going right. Use the photograph as your guide and thread the remaining beads and cherubs. Notice that there is a tiny knot at the beginning and end of each bead section. The space between each bead section is about 1 inch (2.5 cm).

7. When beading is complete, tie the cord ends into a knot. Make certain the necklace can fit over your head.

Earrings

1. For each earring, thread one gold-tone head pin down through the cherub. Clip the head pin, but leave enough wire to form a small loop under the cherub.

2. On another head pin, thread your beads, using the photograph as your guide. At the top of this pin, make another small loop, clip off the excess pin, and join the two loops together. Close tightly, using your needle nose pliers.

Angel Jacket

*If an angel look-
ing over your
shoulder is a
comforting
thought, how
about two angels
on your shoul-
ders? And if a few
kind words about
angels are
appealing, how
about a few
thousand? That's
exactly what
designer Pat
Schieble brought
to life with this
unforgettable
jacket.*

Designer: Pat Schieble

Materials ▾

secondhand jacket or old favorite of your own*

large bottle of squeeze-on acrylic fabric paint

1 yard tightly crinkled fabric, silk and metal blend

scrap of crinkled fabric in a contrasting color

1 block of neutral polymer clay

acrylic paints in flesh color, brown, white, and red

mohair yarn or other material for hair

assortment of thin ribbons

a few small silk flowers

2 miniature musical instruments

1 paper clip

white glue

The designer used a man's sports coat because the construction provides a smooth, sturdy surface to work on.

Tools ▾

oven or toaster oven

hand sewing and sewing machine equipment

sharp craft knife

fine-tipped paint brushes

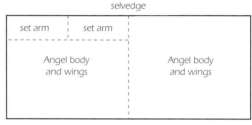

selvedge

set arm | set arm

Angel body and wings | Angel body and wings

Figure 1

Instructions ▾

1. Have the jacket dry cleaned: there are no guarantees after it's decorated.

2. Collect more angel quotations than you think you will need. Start with your favorite ones, then go to *Bartlett's Familiar Quotations*, anthologies on the subject, etc. Regarding the fabric paint, you can choose a contrasting color or match the paint to the jacket so that the writing becomes a textural element in the design (and any mistakes are hidden). Spread the jacket out smoothly on a table and start writing. Begin at the back collar and work your way down; do each side of the front separately. (The paint will need to dry overnight before you turn the jacket over.) Use the grain of the fabric to keep your lettering more or less aligned, or give up and let it wander. Just make whatever you do look deliberate. Take frequent breaks

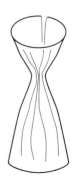

Figure 2

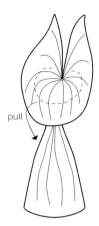

pull

Figure 3

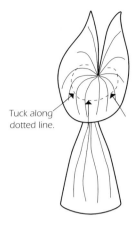

Tuck along dotted line.

Figure 4

Figure 5

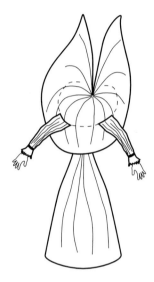

Figure 6

12. Slip the head into position. Sew it securely to the fabric collar; tack the whole thing to the jacket shoulder.

13. Glue on the hair and add the flowers and ribbons.

14. Glue the musical instruments to the hands.

to rest your hand.

You may want to scatter beads, charms, flowers, or other objects across the jacket. Position any large elements first and write around them.

3. Tear the yard of crinkled fabric in half crosswise and ravel the ends for about 1/8 inch (.5 cm). Cut a strip about 2 inches (5 cm) wide along the selvedge of one of the pieces, tear it in half crosswise, and ravel the ends (figure 1).

4. Fold the fabric into a tube. Grasp the tube about three-quarters of the way up and tack it together loosely (figure 2).

5. Holding the tacked point, pull the middle of the upper edge downward to form the wings (figure 3).

6. Make a tuck along the dotted line so that you fashion the wing/bodice/collar. Tack the tuck to the pinch point loosely (figure 4). Now you can see what size to make the angels' faces and hands.

7. From the polymer clay, shape the hands in the position they'll need to hold the musical instruments. (Make sure you have a right and a left hand for each angel.)

8. Shape each clay face with a suggestion of a neck to tuck down into the fabric pinch point. Push half a paper clip into the back of each head to form a loop you can use to tack the head to the fabric.

9. Bake the hands and heads according to package directions.

10. Paint the faces and the hands with acrylics.

11. With a very sharp knife, cut a shallow groove around each wrist. Wrap a small strip of the contrasting fabric around the wrist and tie it in place with thread (figure 5). Tack the middle of the arm assembly up inside the bodice tuck and tack the underside of the bodice down to cover it (figure 6).

Designer:
Jennifer Drake Thomas
Size: 14 x 14 inches
(36 x 36 cm)

Cat Pillow

Despite its pious pose, this cat's coy smile and curled tail suggest that even in heaven, mice and other critters need divine intervention. Designer Jennifer Drake Thomas brought this charmer to life with fabric paints and a love of cats.

Materials ▾

non-bleed fabric paints: blue, white, black, yellow, purple, salmon, and metallic gold

fine-line fabric pens: same colors as above

fabric pens (disappearing transfer type)

2-1/2 yards (28 m) smooth, preshrunk, white cotton fabric or fine muslin for front

2-1/2 yards (28 m) preshrunk, printed or plain fabric for back

14-inch (36 cm) pillow form

2 yards (22 m) cording for pillow piping

matching thread

Tools ▾

hand sewing and sewing machine equipment

fabric paintbrushes: fine-point and 1/2-inch (1.5 cm) flat

Instructions ▾

1. Design and draw the cat angel with bold outlines.

2. Iron the white fabric for the pillow front. Transfer the design using the transfer marker pen.

3. With the fabric flat on a clean surface, paint the robe, being sure to follow the manufacturer's directions. Blend in purple to create shadows and use white to highlight. Try a watercolor-like approach and apply the paint thinly. Paint in the face areas. Delicately shade the areas around the mouth and paws. Go back and add details. Add the gold last to accent the robe and the wings.

For the background, use a generous amount of water with the pigment. Work quickly and loosely. (You may want to practice this on a fabric scrap.)

4. To set the painted design, iron the reverse side of the fabric per manufacturer's directions.

5. To construct the pillow, start by cutting out the front fabric to size, adding 5/8-inch (2 cm) on all sides. Cut out two pieces for the back to make a lapped style. Make the piping by cutting on the bias and basting in place. Pin the front, the two back pieces, and the piping together; stitch using a zipper foot. Trim and turn. Insert the pillow form.

Designer: Patricia Taylor
Size: 12 inches (30.5 cm)

Angel Bear

*Designer Patricia Taylor believes we all need an angel to look out for us, and who
better than a loveable, huggable angel bear!*

Materials ▾

Dream Spinners bear pattern*

fleece in place of cloth (see pattern for
  yardage and supplies)

1/4 yard (23 cm) extra fleece for wings

scraps of cotton for patchwork bear

same amount of silk as fleece for silk bear

metallic thread for silk bear

*Teddy bear pattern: #118, Dream Spinners,
8970 East Hampden Avenue, Denver, Colorado
80231, (800) 474-2665.*

Tools ▾

hand sewing and sewing machine equipment

embroidery needle to fit sewing machine,
  or needles made for use with metallic
  threads (for silk bear)

Patchwork Bear

1. Cut out all the bear pieces and the wings
from the fleece.

2. Using strip piecing method (see step 3)
cover each pattern piece with cotton scraps.
The bears turn out more interesting if you do
this in a random manner; don't make yourself
crazy trying to match the piecing at the seams.

3. To strip piece: Lay the initial fabric piece
on the fleece pattern piece (wrong sides
together). With the right sides together, sew
a second fabric strip or scrap to the first.
Iron open and continue in this manner until
the pattern piece is covered. (Use the silk
setting on your iron so you don't melt the
fleece.) Turn the pattern piece over and cut
away the excess.

4. Follow the pattern directions for constructing and stuffing the bear.

Silk Bear

1. Cut the pattern pieces out of fleece and silk.

2. Match the silk to the fleece piece layer, and machine quilt. You can use your seam guide to sew straight lines; read your sewing machine manual to see if you have one. If you don't have a seam guide, quilt in a random manner.

Hints for using metallic thread: Use an embroidery needle on your machine. There are also special needles sold for use with metallic threads. Set the stitch length longer than usual. As an absolute last resort, loosen the top thread tension.

3. Follow the pattern directions for constructing and stuffing the bear.

Wings

1. Cut two wings out of cloth and one wing out of fleece. Layer the fleece on the bottom with the two cloth wings (right sides together) on top of the fleece.

2. Pin the wings in place and hand stitch them to the bear along the center back and at each shoulder.

▶ *We trust in plumed procession For such the angels go— Rank after Rank, with even feet— And uniforms of Snow.*

EMILY DICKINSON

Flying Angel Bunny

This delightful creature is sure to perk up your Christmas tree or add a bit of fun to a child's bedroom all year 'round.

Designer: Susan McCarson
Size: 7 inches (18 cm)

▶ *It is said, and it is true, that just before we are born a cavern angel puts his finger to our lips and says, "Hush, don't tell what you know." This is why we are born with a cleft on our upper lips and remembering nothing of where we came from.*

RODERICK MACLEISH
PRINCE OMBRA

Materials ▾

8 x 14 inches (20.5 x 36 cm) muslin for body (black or white)

8 x 14 inches (20.5 x 36 cm) calico fabric of your choice for dress

4 x 7 inches (10.5 x 18 cm) quilted muslin for wings

1 x 8-1/2 inches 2.5 x 22 cm) lace

1/4 x 4-1/2 inches (1 x 11.5 cm) elastic

1/2-inch-wide (1.5 cm) ribbon to match calico

1/8-inch-wide (.5 cm) ribbon (for adorning)

embroidery thread in blue and pink

off-white thread

off-white crochet thread

fiberfill

hot glue

Tools ▾

glue gun

hand sewing and sewing machine equipment

5-inch (13 cm) doll sculpture needle

serger (optional)

Instructions ▾

1. Cut out the patterns. Place them on the fabric and cut. Cut the front of the wings from muslin and the back from quilted muslin. The skirt measures 1-1/2 x 8-1/2 inches (4 x 22 cm).

2. Sew the right sides of the head together, leaving a 1/2-inch (1.5 cm) opening at the bottom for stuffing (figure 1).

3. Stuff the ears and head firmly. Hand sew the opening. With blue embroidery thread, make French knots for the eyes. Embroider the nose and mouth with pink thread.

4. Place the legs on the body, matching the arrows (3/16-inch (.75 cm) seam allowance). Place the front and back together and sew, leaving a 1/2-inch (.75 cm) opening at the top of the body (figure 2).

5. Turn the legs and body right side out. Top stitch down the center of the legs to the waist (figure 2). Stuff the legs and body firmly and hand stitch the opening.

6. Place the right sides of the arm cap on the arm, matching the arrows, and sew a 3/16-inch (.75 cm) seam allowance. Place the right sides of the arms and arm cap together and sew, leaving a 1/2-inch (1.5

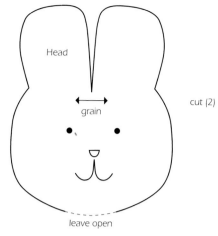

Head

grain

cut (2)

leave open

Figure 1   Enlarge 160%

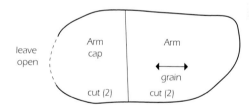

leave open

Body

cut (2)

top stitch

grain   cut (2)

Figure 2   Enlarge 165%

leave open

Arm cap

Arm

grain

cut (2)   cut (2)

Figure 3   Enlarge 160%

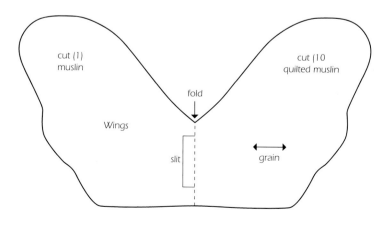

cut (1) muslin

cut (10 quilted muslin

fold

Wings

slit   grain

Figure 4   Enlarge 165%

cm) opening at the top of the arm cap for stuffing (figure 3). Sew the opening.

7. Place the right sides of the wings together and sew all around. With scissors, slit the back of the wings on the muslin side (figure 4). Turn and press with an iron. Fold in half with the muslin sides together. Use a small amount of hot glue to hold (figure 5).

8. With the sculpture needle and crochet thread, sew the arms through the arm caps on either side of the body (figure 6).

9. For the skirt, serge the top and bottom edges, or fold under and sew (figure 7). Sew the lace on the bottom edge. Stretch the elastic and sew to the top of the skirt (use a zigzag stitch). Sew the ends of the skirt together and slip it on the bunny's waist.

10. Glue the 1/2-inch (1.5 cm) ribbon around the waist, over the top of the skirt. Glue the wings on the back of the bunny and glue the head to the body.

11. Add ribbon on the ear and neck.

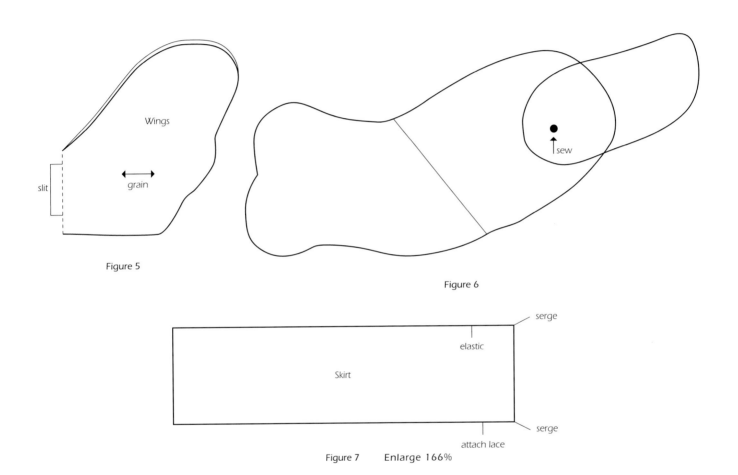

Figure 5

Figure 6

Figure 7   Enlarge 166%

Cat Angel Pins

Artist Susan Kinney suggests that you use your own feline friend for inspiration in making this whimsical purring angel.

Materials ▼

1 block each of white, black, green, and maroon polymer clay

pin backs

instant glue

Tools ▼

oven or toaster oven

clay slicer

brayer

Instructions ▼

1. Knead all the clay to the same consistency.

2. Mix 1/4 block of the black with 1/4 block of the white to make gray.

3. Mix 1/4 block of the maroon with 1/4 block of the white to make pink.

4. Make a very short face cane and wrap it with a thin sheet of black clay for definition.

5. Make a heart-shaped cane, red wrapped in black, and layer the pink clay around it to form the triangular midsection of the cat.

Place this section under the chin, and press.

6. For the wing portion of the cane, make a long bull's-eye log with layers of blue, black, maroon, black, white, and black.

7. Cut one-third of the log and compress it so that it forms an eye shape. Attach slices of this log onto each side of the cat's face to form the wing tops.

8. Cut the remaining log in half. Arrange small slices under the wing tops in a fish-scale pattern.

9. Cut the remaining coil and divide it into four portions. Reduce three of them by rolling them between your hands. Flatten the coils into long shapes, using the photograph as a guide, and arrange

Designer: Susan Kinney
Size: 2 inches (5 cm); 3 inches (7.5 cm)

them to form the rest of the wing cane. Fill in the spaces between the coils with green clay. If you like, you can "marbleize" the green by mixing in bits of black and white.

10. Pack the green color around the head and the entire wing shape. This will help to contain the shape of the cane when you compress it to the desired size.

11. Manipulate the cane into a heart-shaped body, compressing the cane parts as you roll and shape. Make the cane as small and compact as you like.

12. Trim the green from around the head as desired.

13. Slice thin portions off the cane and bake according to the manufacturer's directions.

14. Glue on the pin backs.

Handmade Paper Angels

Designer Claudia Lee creates these whimsical winged ornaments from recycled paper and a lot of imagination.

Designer: Claudia Lee

Size: 4 x 7 inches (10 x 18 cm)

Materials ▾

handmade paper (recipe below)

medium-weight interfacing (available at fabric stores)

acrylic paints in colors of your choice

three-dimensional puffed paints

heavy-weight gold thread

white glue

hot glue

Tools ▾

glue gun

blender

small bucket or bowl

sponge

10-inch (25.5 cm) square fiberglass screening (from hardware store)

paintbrushes

Paper Pulp

1. Collect stationery-quality papers. Remove all the staples and plastic and sort into color families.

2. Tear the paper into pieces, about the size of a quarter, and soak the pieces in water.

3. Fill the blender 3/4 full of water and add about a 1/2 cup (120 ml) of the soaked paper. Pulse-blend until the pulp is the consistency of oatmeal. If the blender begins to sound or smell overworked, remove some of the pulp and continue to blend.

4. Pour the pulp into a colander and let it drain.

5. Repeat steps 3 and 4 until you have enough paper for the project, about 2 cups (.5 liter).

Note: You may use all one color paper or make up several colors and mix them for your project.

Angels

1. Cut the interfacing slightly larger than the finished piece will be. Wet the interfacing and squeeze out the excess water. Place the fabric on your worktable.

2. Trace an angel pattern onto the interfacing if you like, or skip this step and work freehand.

3. Place a handful of soggy pulp (do not wring water out) onto the interfacing and fill in the traced pattern or form your own angel shape.

4. When you're satisfied with the shape, place the fiberglass screen on the angel and place the sponge on the screen.

5. Gently press the sponge-and-screen, and then wring the water from the sponge. Repeat this process, each time increasing the pressure on the sponge until all of the water is removed.

6. Remove the screen and allow the piece to dry thoroughly.

7. When the paper is completely dry, remove it from the interfacing and you are ready to decorate. These angels were painted with acrylics, detailed with puffy black paint, and the stars were painted with gold leaf paint. Because the angels are paper, they can be adorned with ribbons, dried flowers, lace, glitter, in short, anything that can be glued.

8. Make the halo hangers by gluing the gold thread to the back of the head.

▸ *If I have freedom in my love,*
And in my soul am free,
Angels alone that soar above
Enjoy such liberty.

RICHARD LOVELACE

Dog and Cat Angel Boxes

These extraordinary boxes pay tribute to angelic furry favorites. Designed by Beth Palmer, they are decorated with paint, beads, sequins, and love.

Designer: Beth Palmer
Size: 1-1/2 x 3 x 3 inches (4 x 7.5 x 7.5 cm)

Materials ▾

thick paper (marbled, wallpaper, heavy gift wrap)

acrylic paints in your choice of colors

beads

paper scraps

sequins

tiny art objects (flea market finds are great)

sewing thread

white glue

carbon paper

gold and silver paint pens (optional)

spray sealer

Tools ▾

scissors

sewing needle

paintbrush

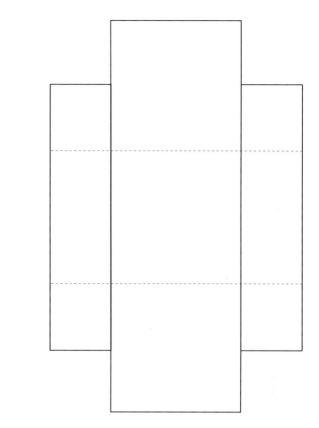

Instructions ▾

1. The center square on the pattern determines the size of the finished box. To make the box shown, enlarge the pattern on a copier or use the graph paper method so that the center square measures 3 x 3 inches (7.5 x 7.5 cm).

2. Transfer your pattern onto the paper you will use and cut out the design. Use paper with substantial body; ordinary paper will be too flimsy.

3. Cut out the boxes and assemble. The box top and bottom are made from the same pattern, so you may wish to make them from different papers.

4. Glue the sides of the boxes with white glue and allow to dry thoroughly.

5. Paint the boxes with acrylic paints (if you have used plain paper).

6. Sew on the beads, glue on bits of decorative paper and wood, and draw designs with the gold and silver paint pens. Glue on the dog and cat figures, and add angel wings. The magic wands shown here are metal scraps; the fish and bone are magazine cutouts.

7. Spray the finished box, inside and out, with spray sealer and allow to dry.

magic pet wand

decorative papers

bead work

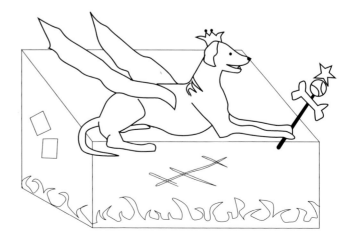

Cornhusk Angels

Despite the apparent sophistication of these singing angels designed by Judy Horn, they are not difficult to make. Use them as lovely mantel or table decorations, or wire them to hang on the tree.

Florals and Naturals

Designer: Judy Horn
Size: 3 x 11 inches (7.5 x 28 cm)

Materials ▾

2 ounces (60 g) of cornhusks

heavy-, medium-, and fine-gauge floral
wire

3/4-inch-diameter (2 cm) foam ball

dried corn silk

white glue

hot glue

masking tape

sage green fabric dye or color of your
choice

Tools ▾

scissors

wire cutters

glue gun

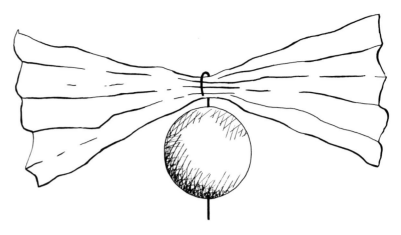

Figure 1

Instructions ▾

1. To make green husks, prepare a solution of sage green fabric dye, double strength, and soak the husks until they are the desired color. They should be flexible and easy to handle. If not, dilute the dye bath and continue to soak the husks until they're pliable.

2. Soak the remaining husks in a bucket of water for 15 to 30 minutes, until they're easy to separate, bend, and fold.

3. Cut a 3-inch (8 cm) piece of heavy wire and make a fishhook in one end. Insert the other end into the foam ball.

4. Cut a piece of cornhusk about 2 inches (5 cm) wide and 4 inches (12 cm) long. Gather it in the middle. Place it on top of the ball and pull the wire until the hook is all the way into the foam, trapping the gathered husk in the center and fastening it to the ball (figure 1). Spread the husk over the ball to cover it; you now have the head. Twist a piece of fine-gauge wire around the neck (figure 2).

5. Now for the arms. Cut a 6-inch (15 cm) piece of medium-gauge wire and place it lengthwise along one side of a cornhusk that's about 7 inches (18 cm) long and 3 inches (4 cm) wide. Roll the husk snugly around the wire. Tie the center of this cylinder with fine-gauge wire. Trim the husk ends so the cylinder is 6 inches (15 cm) long (figure 3).

6. To make the sleeves, gather a 3-inch square of cornhusk around one arm about 1/2 inch (1 cm) from one end and tie it

Figure 2

Figure 3

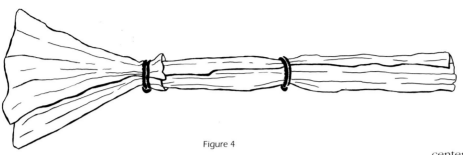

Figure 4

Figure 5

with fine wire (figure 4). Turn the husk inside out, back toward the center of the cylinder. Tie the sleeve at the center of the arm with fine wire (figure 5). Repeat on the other side to make the other sleeve.

7. Position the arms an appropriate distance below the head and wire them to the center "backbone" wire.

8. For the bodice, cut two pieces of husk (use green if you're making the green angel) 1-1/4 inches (3 cm) wide and about 3 inches (4 cm) long. To avoid unfinished edges, fold each long side to the center, so that each strip is 3/4 inch (2 cm) wide. Lay the center of each strip on a shoulder and bring the ends down the front and back, crossing at the waist in both front and back. Wrap a piece of fine wire around the waist and twist the wire ends together.

9. To make the skirt, first bend the arms up out of your way. Using your largest and best-looking husk first (use green for this step if you're making a green angel), place four to six large husks evenly around the chest and head, gathering the husks into soft folds as you go. Overlap the waist wire by about 1/2 inch (1.5 cm) (figure 6). Wrap a piece of fine wire around the waist. Gently fold each husk down, tugging and shaping once the husk is right side out. Trim the bottom of the skirt with scissors to make it even.

10. Reposition the arms while they're still wet, arranging them so the angel will be ready to hold sheet music. Allow to dry completely, about four days.

11. For angel hair, spread white glue on the head and wrap the corn silk around the head. Glue down or trim any flyaway silks; no angel should have a bad-hair day.

12. Glue two large husks together to make one thick one, using craft glue, and allow to dry. Cut out a pair of wings and some sheet music and hot-glue them into place.

13. Cut a 2-inch (5 cm) piece of heavy-gauge wire and wrap it with masking tape. Bend it into a halo and insert it into the back of the angel's head.

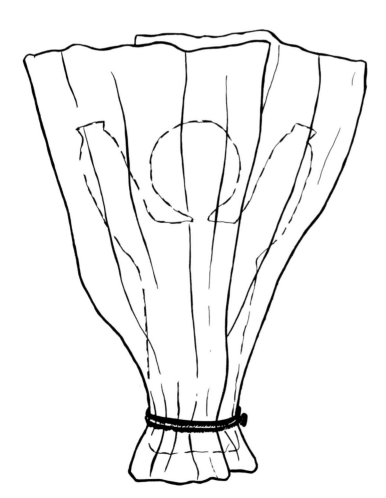

Figure 6

Designer: Michelle West
Size: 18 inches (46 cm)

Golden Cherub Swag

Designer Michelle West achieves a dramatic effect by topping a bold arrangement of dried flowers with a vibrant, gold angel head.

Materials ▾

assorted dried flowers (caspia, German statice, and eucalyptus)
fine- and medium-gauge floral wire
purchased cherub head (with a wire or hole for hanging)

Tools ▾

scissors
wire cutters

Instructions ▾

1. To make each side of the swag, arrange your dried flowers into a generous bunch and wire it together with the fine-gauge floral wire. If you need to layer the flowers, simply attach the top layers to the bottom layers with the wire.

2. With the medium-gauge wire, join the two swag sides together.

3. Attach the cherub head to the swag with the medium-gauge wire.

4. Make a hanger out of medium-gauge wire attached to the back of the piece.

Winged Wreath

Designed by Barbara Applebaum, the gauzy wings on this gorgeous wreath and the delicate colors of the flowers evoke the sweetness and grace of cherubs in flight.

Designer: Barbara Applebaum

Size: 13 x 24 inches (33.5 x 62 cm)

Materials ▾

14-inch (36 cm) wire wreath base

8-inch (20.5) white pipe cleaner

2 yards (92.5 cm) pink tulle, 60 inches (152 cm) wide

2 yards (92.5 cm) metallic gold craft cord with stars

(19) 3-inch (7.5 cm) bunches and (12) 7-inch (18 cm) bunches of dried flowers: baby's breath, sea lavender, caspia (white and purple), and florets of silver-king artemisia

3 pink silk carnations

2 white silk roses

8 dried zinnias (pink and purple)

10 dried larkspur (pink and blue)

15 dried white yarrow (sprayed pink and light lavender)

several stems of dried statice (purple and deep pink)

10 lemon leaves, a few sprayed gold

4 milkweed pods sprayed gold

7 small hydrangea (pink or blue tones)

1 small cherub head with wings

2 small cherubs

hot glue

gold spray paint

Tools ▾

thin-, medium-, and heavy-gauge steel wire

wire cutters

white floral tape

glue gun

Instructions ▾

1. Make an oval frame from a 14-inch (36 cm) wreath base by pushing in the sides slightly.

2. Bend the thin-gauge wire into two loops for the wings and attach them to the top third of the wreath form with medium-gauge wire. Cover the wire wings, the wreath base, and the attachment wire with white floral tape.

3. Make a hanger by folding the pipe cleaner in half and attaching it to the back of the base.

4. The top third of the wreath is covered with the 3-inch (7.5 cm) bunches of dried flowers. The lower two-thirds is covered with the 7-inch (18 cm) bunches. Hold each bunch together with white floral tape and attach it to the wire base with medium-gauge wire. Be sure to cover the previous stems with newly attached bunches until you have completely covered the base.

5. Decorate the flower-covered base by gluing on the other flowers listed, using the photograph as a guide.

6. Glue on the cherub head in the bottom center of the wreath and glue on the two smaller angels to either side. Glue on two gold lemon leaves behind the cherub's head.

7. Fold the tulle in half and drape it over the wings. Wrap some of the tulle around the wire and leave some loose. Loosely wrap the gold cord around the tulle to shape and decorate the wings.

> ▸ *It is not because angels are holier than men or devils that makes them angels, but because they do not expect holiness from one another, but from God alone.*
>
> WILLIAM BLAKE

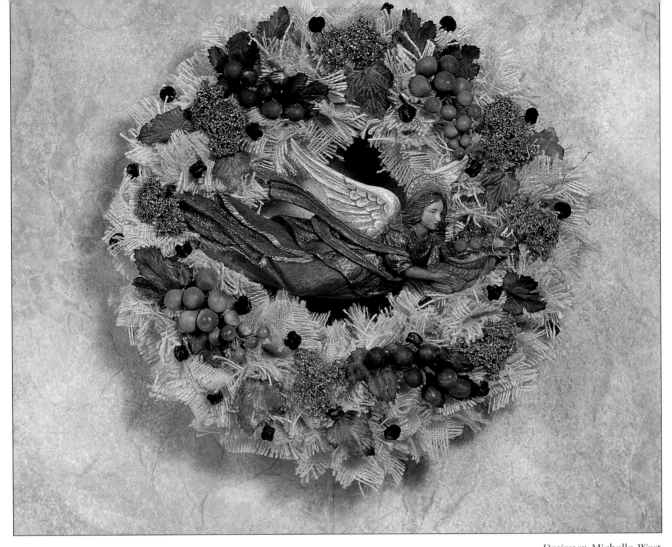

Designer: Michelle West
Size: 14 inches (36 cm)

Burlap Angel Wreath

This simple-to-make wreath, designed by Michelle West, is a glorious marriage of subtle color and varied texture.

Materials ▾

14-inch (36 cm) foam wreath base

6 yards (6 m) 2-inch (5 cm) cream-colored paper ribbon

1/2 yard (.5 m) undyed burlap

hot glue

artificial grapes and berries

dried flowers

artificial leaves (extra grape leaves are nice)

purchased angel for centerpiece

Tools ▾

2-1/2-inch (6.5 cm) natural wood picks

glue gun

scissors

Instructions ▾

1. Cover the wreath form with the ribbon, overlapping each round.

2. Cut the burlap into 4-inch (10.4 cm) squares. Pinch each square in the middle and wrap the wire part of the wood pick around the pinch. Wire tightly. Touch the center pieces with a bit of hot glue to keep them secure.

3. Using the photograph as your guide, stick the burlap squares on the wreath form. Make sure to cover the sides as well.

4. Ravel the edges of the burlap squares, as shown in the picture, until you get the look you want.

5. Pick in the berries and grapes.

6. Glue on the leaves and dried flowers.

7. Glue on the angel.

Designer: Michelle West
Size: 14 x 30 inches (36 x 77 cm)

Raffia Angel

To craft this graceful angel, designer Michelle West used simple, inexpensive materials in imaginative ways.

Materials ▾

purchased raffia doll base 30 inches (77 cm) tall

small heart-shaped grapevine wreath

silk pine needles

dried flowers

pearl or gold beads

airy wired gold ribbon

wired white ribbon

lace scraps

gold cord

hot glue

Tools ▾

glue gun

scissors

Instructions ▾

1. Cut the doll's arms apart from each other and glue the heart-shaped wreath into her hands.

2. Pull some of the doll's hair from the pony tail and spread the hair over her shoulders to give her a flowing look.

3. Glue lace around the doll's neck to make a ruffled collar.

4. Make wings from airy wired gold ribbon and attach the wings to her back.

5. Twine gold ribbon, white ribbon, and gold cord around the angel's arms and hands, and bend the ribbon into spirals.

6. Make the halo from silk pine needles, gold cord, and tiny pearl beads. Hot glue the halo to her head.

7. Make her an angelic necklace from a string of tiny pearls.

8. Complete her outfit by gluing tiny dried flowers or herbs on her wreath and in her hands.

Herb and Flower Angel

This fragrant and colorful angel is easy to make and will add a charming touch to any room in the house. Use herbs and flowers from your own garden to give your creation a personal touch.

Designer: Dolly Lutz Morris

Size: 6 x 10 inches (15.5 x 25.5 cm)

Materials ▾

dried flowers (roses, tansy, astilbe, lavender, pink and white yarrow, baby's breath, goldenrod, feverfew, Spanish moss)

hot glue

twine

12-inch-long (30.5 cm) birch twigs

floral wire

corn husks

6-inch (15.5 cm) mini broom

2-inch (5 cm) twig wreath

1-inch (2.5 cm) wooden bead for head

red and black permanent markers

powder blush

Tools ▾

wire cutters

glue gun

Instructions ▾

1. Using the glue gun, attach the wooden head bead to the top of the broom.

2. To make arms, center a 3/4 x 5-inch (2 x 13 cm) length of corn husk onto the back of the broom and attach it with glue. Bring the ends of the husk around to the front of the figure and glue them in place, using the photograph as a guide.

3. Make the angel wings by shaping several 12-inch (30.5 cm) birch twigs into a "figure eight" pattern. Wire the twigs together in the center to secure. Attach the wings to the back of the angel with wire.

4. With permanent markers, draw a simple face on the wooden head. Apply powder blush to the angel's cheeks. Glue Spanish moss to the top of the head to create hair.

5. Using your glue gun to attach the flowers, fashion the skirt by first attaching long strands or sprays in more muted colors. Lavender, astilbe, and goldenrod make a good bottom layer. Next, add yarrow and tansy.

6. Glue the twig wreath to the ends of the arms, and cover the wreath with the bright rosebuds.

7. Glue yarrow and feverfew to the shoulders and baby's breath to the wings.

8. Make a hanger by tying a piece of twine to the back of the angel.

Designer: Dolores Muller
Size: 6-1/2 inches (16.5 cm)

Star Garland Angel

Designer Dolores Muller created a beautiful wheat angel like this one for the 1993 White House Christmas tree. It will add a first class touch to your tree, too.

Materials ▾

18 wheat straws with long heads*

25 wheat straws with heads removed

12 inches (31 cm) gold craft cord with stars

24 inches (61.5 cm) of 1/4-inch-wide (1 cm) gold ribbon

beige carpet or button hole thread

1 gold snowflake-shaped sequin

6 inches (15.5 cm) of #28 wire

hot glue

water

*Wheat straws: Campus Granary, Bethel College Women's Assoc., N. Newton, KS 67117

Tools ▾

pointed scissors

ruler

wire clipper

glue gun

comb with wide-spaced teeth

Clove Hitch Knot

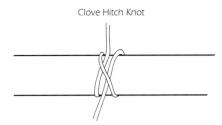

Figure 1

Figure 2

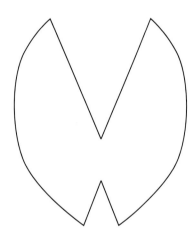

Figure 3

Instructions ▾

1. Before you begin to weave, it is essential that you learn to make a clove hitch knot. In straw work, whenever a tie is indicated, the clove hitch knot is used. To make a clove hitch knot, hold the wheat horizontally in your left hand. Place the thread under your left thumb on the front of the wheat, leaving about 4 inches (10.5 cm) hanging down. With your right hand, bring the other end around the back of the wheat and to the right of the end hanging. Make a second loop around the wheat, toward the back, and to the left of the hanging end in front. Put the end through the second loop and pull both ends tight. Tie an over-hand knot to finish off (figure 1).

2. Before you begin to weave, clean the straw as follows: Cut the straw above the first joint and slide the leaf sheaf away (see figure 2 for the different parts of a wheat stem). Select 43 wheat straws with matching long heads and stems. Cut the heads off 25 straws just below the neck. Soak the wheat in warm water for 1/2 - 2 hours; the wheat is ready to weave when the stem is pliable.

3. To make the arms, take five straws without heads and cut them 5 inches long (13 cm). Insert a 6-inch (15.5 cm) wire through one of the straws. Place the straw with the wire in the middle of the other four straws. Holding the straws between your thumb and index finger, tie tightly in the center so the five straws stay flat and fan out. Make two more ties 1/4 inch (1 cm) from each end, again keeping the straws flat. Bend the arms halfway between the center and each end-tie. Trim the excess wire.

4. For the wings, take 15 straws without heads and cut them approximately 6 inches long (15.5 cm). Tie tightly in the center while holding the straws between your thumb and index finger so they lay flat and fan out. Trim into a wing shape (figure 3).

5. For the body and skirt of the angel, use the 18 wheat straws with heads. Measure and cut stems 8 inches (20.5 cm) from the neck. Gather the wheat together so the necks of the straws are uniform. Measure 3 inches (7.5 cm) from the neck and tie.

Divide the straws evenly at the cut ends and slip an 8-inch (20.5 cm) piece of gold ribbon uniformly in between.

6. To form the angel's head, bend the straws with the wheat heads evenly down over the tie you just made; tie again 1/2 inch (1.5 cm) down. Make a hanger now by tying a knot at the end of the ribbon.

7. Insert the arms under five straws just below the angel's neck. Slip the wings under three straws in the back. Tie gold ribbon 3/4 inch (2 cm) down from the neck, forming the waist.

The body of the angel is now complete.

8. To fashion the skirt, place the angel on a flat surface and arrange the straw heads evenly and slightly flared. Place a book, or any heavy object, on the heads to keep them flat while drying. It takes 2 to 3 days for the wheat to dry completely.

9. After the angel is dry, trim the beards of the wheat evenly along the bottom.

10. Use three straws to weave the ribbon trim for the angel's skirt. (This pattern is known as the "cat-foot.") Tie together at the small ends. Spread the straws out to form a Y (figure 4a). Hold them between the thumb, second, and third finger, just below the tie. Fold straw A to the left side of B (figure 4b). Fold straw B over to the former position of A (figure 4c). Fold straw C up and to the right of A (figure 4d). Fold A down to the former position of C (figure 4e). Repeat from the beginning until 4 - 5 inches (10 - 13 cm) of the pattern has been woven. Tie and trim.

11. To make the rose, take one straw and split it lengthwise with pointed scissors. Open the straw with your fingers and run your nail along its inside several times to flatten it. Fold the straw 2 inches (5 cm) from the wide end, to make a right angle (figure 6a). Fold again at a right angle (figure 6b), leaving a space in between. Fold at a right angle again (figure 6c). Turn the piece counter-clockwise as you fold, so as to be always folding downward. Continue folding in this manner, making 16 folds in all. Tuck the end of the straw into the hole formed in the center. Pull down tightly, and while holding the two ends under the rose in your left hand, gently turn the petals clockwise to create the spiral of the rose petals. Tie the ends closely under the rose. Trim the ends close to the tie.

12. The leaf, or spreuer, is made by splitting and flattening a straw, as you did for the rose. Insert the wide end of the straw between the second and third teeth of the comb, from the back, so the end points toward you. Bend the straw up the front of the comb and insert it between the fifth and sixth teeth (figure 7a).

Bring the straw behind and down to the starting point. Next, bring the straw up the front of the comb, covering the center end of the leaf, and insert it between the fourth and fifth teeth on the left side of the center (figure 7b). Repeat the technique to the right of the center point. Repeat left and right until there are three points on both sides of the center, finishing so the end of the straw is at the back

Catfoot Pattern

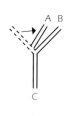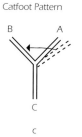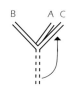

a b c d e

Figure 4

Rose

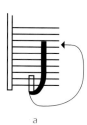

a b c

Figure 5

Leaf

a b c

Figure 6

of the comb. To tie off, turn the comb over and take the end of the straw down between the first and second teeth, through all the sections from right to left, and then back through the loop to the bottom, and pull tight (figure 7c). Remove the leaf from the comb.

13. After all the parts are dry, you are ready to assemble the angel. Use hot glue to fasten the woven "catfoot" ribbon to the angel's skirt where the stems meet the heads and trim the excess. Glue the leaf and rose over the ends. Glue the sequin to the back of the head to create a halo. Make a sash around the waist with the gold ribbon, and complete your angel by fastening the gold craft cord to each hand.

Painted Wood

Designer: Terry Taylor

Size: 8 inches (20.5 cm)

Winged Candlestick

To create this handsome piece, designer Terry Taylor used a style of ornate wood carving called tramp art. *This craft was popular in America from about 1875 to 1930, and artists (not tramps!) often whittled cigar boxes and fruit crates.*

Materials ▾

(1) 4 x 4 x 12-inch (10.5 x 10.5 x 31 cm) block of basswood cut as follows:

    (1) 1-3/8 x 1-3/8 x 8 inches (3.75 x 3.75 x 20.5) - I*

    (1) 1/2 x 2 x 2 inches (1.5 x 5 x 5 cm) - II

    (1) 1/2 x 2-3/4 x 2-3/4 inches (1.5 x 7 x 7 cm) - III

(1) 1/4 x 3 x 18-inches (1 x 7.5 x 46 cm) sheet of plywood

(1) #6 1-1/2-inches (4 cm) wood screw

upholstery tacks

acrylic primer

acrylic paint or gold composition leaf

acrylic antiquing glaze

acrylic varnish (gloss)

The block of basswood is enough for two candlesticks and is available in hobby shops; any soft, white wood such as pine or poplar will work.

Tools ▾

carpenter's glue

carving knife

drill press or drill

table saw or jigsaw

furniture clamp (to expand to 10 inches)

3/4-inch (2 cm) wood borer or drill bit

Instructions ▾

1. Cut wood according to dimensions provided (I, II, and III).

2. Cut two large wings and four small wings (figures 1 and 2) from the sheet of plywood.

3. Mark the center top of piece I using a 3/4-inch (2 cm) drill bit or wood borer and drill a 3/4-inch-deep (2 cm) hole for the candle.

4. Mark the centers of pieces II and III and drill a small hole in each as a guide hole for the wood screw.

5. Sand all edges smooth.

6. Use a carving or pocketknife to make v-cuts on the edges of these three pieces. To do this, make a shallow, straight cut about 1/8 inch (.5 cm) deep, and then angle the knife at either side to complete the v-cut. Use a scrap of wood to practice on until you are comfortable with the technique.

7. On edges A-B on the small wing parts (figure 1) make v-cuts as in step 6. Do not make the other cuts yet.

8. Position a small wing (figure 1) onto a large wing (figure 2); glue, clamp, and allow to dry. Repeat on the opposite side.

9. Sand the top edges of the wings smooth.

10. Make v-cuts on all edges of the wings except for edge C-D. Push or tap the upholstery tacks onto the upper portion of the wings on both sides.

11. Drive the screw into piece III and allow the tip to poke up just a bit. Put glue on the bottom of piece II. Set this piece on the tip of the screw; align it, clamp, and let dry.

12. Drive the screw until the tip protrudes a bit. Put glue on the bottom of piece I; align it on the screw tip, clamp, and allow to dry. Position the upholstery tacks on the two opposite sides, and drive them into place.

13. Spread glue on edge C-D. Position it on the candlestick, clamp, and let dry. Repeat this with the other wing.

14. Prime the candlestick with acrylic primer and allow to dry. Gold acrylic paint may be used now or follow the manufacturer's directions for gold composition leaf (used on the piece shown here). Once the desired color is achieved, allow the candlestick to dry. Coat with acrylic varnish. A rubbed finish with acrylic antiquing glaze gives an aged look and further defines the carved edges. Allow the glaze to dry, and finish with a final coat of gloss varnish.

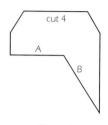

Figure 1

Enlarge 220%

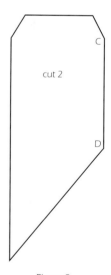

Figure 2

Enlarge 220%

Catcher-in-the-Sky Angel Table

With a bow to Lord Byron and J.D. Salinger, designer Pat Schieble turned an old end table into an eye-pleasing (and poetic) heirloom using simple painting techniques and an acrobatic imagination.

On the table legs, Pat has hand painted this verse from Byron: *"The angels all were singing out of tune, and hoarse from having little else to do, excepting to wind up the sun and moon, or curb a runaway young star or two."* And who better to catch a runaway star than Holden Caulfield, the immortal young hero of Salinger's book, *The Catcher in the Rye.*

Designer: Pat Schieble
Size: 1 foot wide, 2 feet long, 2 feet tall (31 x 61.5 x 61.5 cm)

Materials ▾

end table with curved leg supports

mineral spirits

enamel primer

latex enamel: khaki, sky blue, white, and brown

acrylic gold and silver leaf

Tools ▾

sandpaper

paintbrushes

Instructions ▾

1. Clean the table with mineral spirits and sand it lightly.

2. Paint on a base coat of khaki latex enamel and let dry.

3. Brush on an irregular coat of sky blue latex enamel, and work in some cloud shapes with white latex enamel while the blue is still wet.

4. Paint the two angels on the leg supports and add the verse. Then paint the young angel catching the shooting stars. (Or create your own one-of-a-kind angel design.)

Musical Angel Table

This impressive table began life plain and unadorned, but its form spoke strongly to designer Pat Schieble: angels, it said. The technique she used to shape the musical messengers would work on similar tables that harbor invisible angels.

Designer: Pat Schieble
Size: 1 foot wide, 2 feet long, 2 feet tall (30.5 x 61.5 x 61.5 cm)

> ▶ *The angels sing the praise of their Lord and ask forgiveness for those on earth.*
>
> THE KORAN

Materials ▾

wooden table with 4 legs (preferably with a 3-tier design)

enamel primer

latex enamel paints of your choice

acrylic gold leaf

posterboard

sheet of thin fiberboard

mineral spirits

white glue

brads

Tools ▾

sandpaper

saber saw

paintbrushes

craft knife

Instructions ▾

1. Clean the table with mineral spirits.

2. Gild the top and shelf edges.

3. Sketch the shape of the angel onto posterboard and cut it out. Use this as a pattern to cut four angels from the fiberboard using a saber saw. Attach the angels with glue and brads. (The designer created angel shapes with a 90-degree angle to take advantage of the table's odd configuration. As a result, she placed opposite shoulder and elbow joints on the corner so that the face and hands could point in opposite directions.)

4. Prime the angels and paint them, following the design in the photograph or creating your own.

Carved Angel

This remarkable angel, carved by David Vance, has a timeless magic to it. The kindly face puts one in mind of Saint Nicholas, Moses, Father Time, or perhaps a beloved grandfather.

Materials ▾

limb of white pine tree (or any soft wood)

(2) 1/4-inch (1 cm) wood strips for wings

aluminum sheeting

screws

white latex enamel

latex enamel paints of your choice

optional: walnut stain and matte or clear acrylic spray sealer

Tools ▾

sanding drum

flexible shaft carver

hand-held electric tool with small carving and sanding bits

sharp carving knife

band saw

fine-grit sandpaper

paintbrush

Instructions ▾

1. Find your piece of wood to carve. You can use a curved or straight limb.

2. Strip the bark from the limb with a sanding drum and a flexible shaft carver. If the wood is green, stripping the bark allows it to dry faster. (Bark from dry wood is much easier to remove.) Don't worry about the cracks that appear as the wood dries: work these into the design.

3. As you carve, remove as little wood as possible. Keep it simple. Many details can be added with paint.

4. Sand the wood with fine sandpaper and give it a base coat of white latex enamel. When dry, lightly sand to remove the wood that will fuzz up.

5. Now you can paint the angel. To achieve an antique look, lightly sand the piece so that small amounts of the base coat and wood show through. Stain with a walnut stain. Wipe away the excess and spray with a matte or satin clear acrylic sealer.

6. With a band saw, cut the wings from 1/4-inch (1 cm) wood strips and carve them with a sanding drum. Paint them; when dry, screw them into position on the back.

7. Cut a halo from the aluminum sheeting and paint it gold. When dry, screw it onto the head.

▶ *None sing so wildly well As the angel Israfel And the giddy stars (so legends tell) Ceasing their hymns, attend the spell Of his voice, all mute.*

Edgar Allan Poe

Designer: David Vance

Size: 15 inches (38.5 cm)

Rocking Angels

These charming wooden angels, designed by Elaine Knoll, have a folk-art quality that makes them both appealing and timeless.

Designer: Elaine Knoll
Size: 8 x 8-3/4 inches (20.5 x 22.5 cm)

Materials ▾

any wood:

> (1) 3/4 x 6 x 6 inches (2 x 15.5 x 15.5 cm) for angel

> (2) 3/4 x 2-1/2 x 2-1/2 inches (2 x 6.5 x 6.5 cm) for stars

> (1) 1-1/2 x 2 x 8 inches (4 x 5 x 20.5 cm) for rocker

(3) 1/4 x 1-3/4-inch (1 x 4.5 cm) dowels

acrylic base coat (off-white)

acrylic paints in colors of your choice

water base varnish

wood glue

Tools ▾

band saw

drill with 1/4-inch (1 cm) bit

sandpaper

paintbrushes

Instructions ▾

1. Trace the pattern pieces onto the wood and cut out.

2. Drill 1/4-inch (1 cm) holes in the center of all the pieces where the dowels will be placed in step 11.

3. Apply a base coat to all the pieces, front and back. Note: these angels are painted on the front, back and sides. Let dry and sand lightly.

4. Paint the face and sides of the head with a flesh color.

5. Sketch in the hairline and paint on the hair.

6. You can leave the face blank or paint in features.

7. Paint the body, sides, and back one color.

8. Sketch in the arms, hands, halo, and collar, and then paint.

9. Paint the wings and stars.

10. When dry, finish all the pieces with a clear satin water base varnish. Optional: an antiquing medium can be applied over the varnish and wiped off for a desired effect.

11. Glue the three dowels into the rocker and glue the angel and stars onto the dowels.

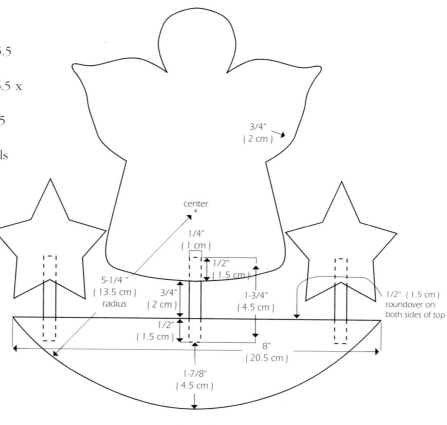

Figure 1

Enlarge 200%

▶ *Ring out ye crystal spheres,*

Once bless our human ears

(If ye have power to touch our senses so)

And let your silver chime

Move in melodious time;

And let the base of heav'n's deep organ blow,

And with your ninefold harmony

Make up full consort to th' angelic symphony.

JOHN MILTON

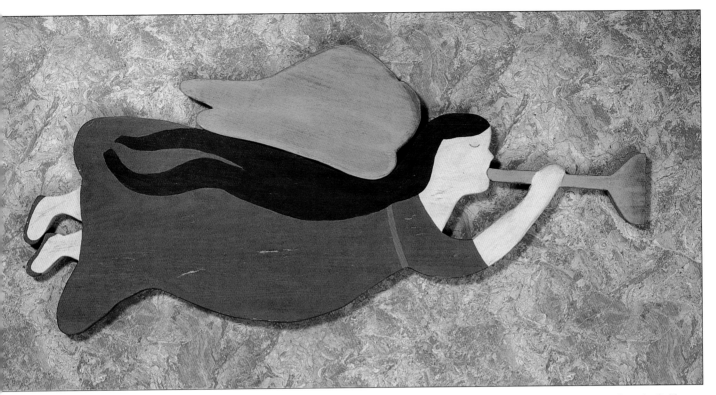

Designer: Bonnie S. Troyer
Size: 8 x 14 inches (20.5 x 36 cm)

Primitive Guardian Angel

Bonnie Troyer's simple wooden angel comes by its aged look naturally; it has graced the front of a friend's house for years.

Materials ▾

3/4 x 12 x 45-inch (2 x 31 x 115.5 cm) wood, any type

medium- and fine-grit sandpaper

acrylic paints in colors of your choice

white glue

(2) 1/2 x 2-inch (1.5 x 5 cm) metal brackets

(8) 1/4-inch (1 cm) wood screws

sawtooth picture hanger

Tools ▾

jigsaw

screwdriver

paintbrushes

Instructions ▾

1. Using grid paper, enlarge the pattern until the angel is the size you want.

2. Trace the pattern onto the wood with a pencil. Using the jigsaw, cut out the angel and the trumpet as one piece. Cut out the wing separately.

3. Sand smooth all the surfaces, paying careful attention to the edges.

4. Using the pattern as your guide, pencil in the angel's dress, slippers, hair, and trumpet.

5. Paint the angel and the wing. Allow the paint to dry, and then apply a second coat.

6. Using medium-grit sandpaper, lightly sand some surfaces and some edges to achieve an antique look.

7. Glue the wing onto the angel and allow it to dry thoroughly.

8. Using the wood screws, attach the brackets to the wing and angel so that the two pieces are securely joined.

9. Attach the sawtooth hanger to the back of the angel.

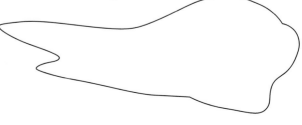

144
▼

Carved Angel Headboard

Your little ones will be eager to go to sleep with this beautiful guardian angel to watch over them. Artist Tom Schulz built and painted this celestial companion for his four-year-old nephew.

Materials ▾

4 x 8-foot (123.5 x 247 cm) piece plywood (sign quality)

(2) 2 x 2 x 54-inch (5 x 5 x 138.5 cm) pieces solid oak stock

(5) 3/16 x 2 x 60-inch (.75 x 5 x 154 cm) pieces solid oak stock

1 small container copper weatherstripping brads

(100) 1-5/8-inch (4.25 cm) Phillips self-tapping drywall screws

(8) 3/8-inch (1.3 cm) oak plugs

carpenter's wood glue

stencil paper or plastic

acrylic paints: burnt sienna, ultramarine blue, and white, or latex enamel house paint tinted with artist's colors

clear spray varnish

spray paint: flat white, flat black, and gold

latex primer

acrylic glazing medium

Designer: Tom Schulz

Size: 42-1/4 x 52-1/2 inches (108.5 x 134.5 cm)

Tools ▾

craft knife

hammer

Phillips-head screwdriver

power drill

3/8-inch (1.3 cm) drill bit

3/8-inch (1.3 cm) countersink bit

jigsaw

orbital sander

120-grit paper for orbital sander

table saw with dado blade or router with
    3/4-inch (2 cm) rabbet bit

220-grit sandpaper

paintbrushes

circular saw

Instructions ▾

1. Using a copy machine or the graph paper method, enlarge your angel design. Trace the design onto the stencil paper and cut the stencil out with the craft knife.

2. In each of the two oak stock pieces, cut a 3/4-inch (2 cm) dado which is 3/8 inch (1.3 cm) deep and runs the length of the piece. Set aside.

3. Measure and cut a rectangle 36 x 40 inches (92.5 x 103 cm) from the plywood. You will have enough plywood left for another headboard. Using a compass or a pencil and string, find the center of the rectangle and draw an arc across the top, or short side, of the rectangle. This will create the rounded top of the headboard.

4. Trace the halo circle onto the headboard, centering the design and pressing very lightly on your pencil; sign quality plywood is quite soft. Do not cut the circle. Instead, place the angel head stencil onto the circle until the angel is where you want it. Then trace the top of the angel's head within the circle. This design forms your halo cut.

5. Drill a pilot hole somewhere inside your halo cut and cut out the halo using the jigsaw.

6. Slide the grooved legs onto the plywood piece, and have each leg extend 2 inches (5 cm) above the side of the plywood. Finished legs will measure about 45-3/4 inches (117.5 cm) tall. Continue the arc of the top of the headboard down across the leg pieces. Remove the leg pieces and cut the legs across your mark with a jigsaw. Legs and plywood should form one clean arc.

▶ There are four corners on my bed, There are four angels at my head, Matthew, Mark, Luke, and John, Bless the bed I sleep on.

A Child's Prayer

7. Using first glue and then weatherstripping nails, attach the thin oak strips to the top of the bed one at a time, allowing some drying time between each strip. The strips will hang out beyond the headboard. Attach all five strips using five or six nails per strip. Trim the edges of the strips so that the edges are smooth and even with the edge of the plywood. Allow the piece to set overnight.

8. Using the orbital sander and the 120-grit paper, sand the entire headboard, paying particular attention to the edges.

9. Paint the plywood section with two coats of latex primer, allowing drying time between coats.

10. Using the flat black spray paint, transfer the angel face pattern onto the board. Arrange the wing stencils in a pleasing manner and paint them onto the board. When the black paint is set (but not necessarily dry), repeat this process using the gold paint. This softens the lines.

11. Paint everything outside the stencil with a light sky blue.

Paint the angel's face with white mixed with burnt sienna to achieve the desired flesh tone. Paint in the details using full-strength artist's color mixed with a bit of glazing medium. Add shadows, dark areas, and facial details. Create clouds by spritzing the top area of the headboard with white spray paint. After all paint detailing is done, allow the piece to dry thoroughly, two to three days.

12. Put carpenter's glue in each dado and attach the legs to the plywood. Allow the glue to dry. Secure the legs to the headboard by drilling three pilot holes through each leg and into the plywood. Using the drywall screws, attach the legs, and then fill the screw holes by setting in the oak plugs.

13. Sand the entire headboard lightly with 220-grit sandpaper.

14. Coat the piece with clear varnish and sand again with 220-grit sandpaper. Repeat this step as many times as you like; the more coats of varnish, the deeper and richer the piece will appear.

15. If you like, you can tape or staple a short strand of tree lights to the back of the bed above the angel's halo. The angel will appear luminescent, and your child will have a night-light.

Angelic Magazine Holder

Designer Mary Jane Miller likes to paint angels on all types of furniture. Here she performs her celestial magic on an old magazine holder.

Designer: Mary Jane Miller
Size: 14 x 16 inches (36 x 41 cm)

Materials ▾

white acrylic house paint
acrylic artist paints in colors of your choice
polyurethane finish

Tools ▾

sandpaper
paintbrushes

Instructions ▾

1. With sandpaper, slightly rough up the surface of the wood.

2. Give the piece a base coat with the white house paint.

3. When dry, paint the angel design and other details with acrylic artist paints.

4. When dry, give it two coats of polyurethane finish.

Thomas Wolfe's Angel

In 1949, this angel was identified as "the angel" of Thomas Wolfe's well-known novel, *Look Homeward, Angel*, first published in 1929. Purchased by the Johnson family of Hendersonville, North Carolina, the beautiful angel marks the grave of Margaret Bates Johnson who died in 1905. Hendersonville is close to Asheville where Wolfe spent his childhood, and which, renamed Altamont, is the novel's locale.

Although several angels graced the porch of Wolfe's father's marble shop over the years, the angel found in Oakdale Cemetery is the only one that matches Wolfe's description: "…it had come from Carrara, in Italy, and it held a stone lily delicately in one hand. The other hand was lifted in benediction."

As a boy, Thomas appeared to be as smitten with these angels as was his father, who purchased them at great expense and had them shipped from Italy. The stonecutter in *Look Homeward, Angel*, never learned to carve an angel's head, much as he longed to. The spirit of this gentle angel has been captured forever in stone and in words.

Wings Around the World

This lovely stained glass, designed by Martha Mitchell, suggests that the helping power of angels is indeed far-reaching.

*Tin,
Wire,
and Glass*

Designer: Martha Mitchell

Size: 7 inches (18 cm) diameter

149

Enlarge 178%

Materials ▾

carbon paper

glue stick

copperfoil

black patina (optional)

flux

solder (50/50 or 60/40)

blue opak glass or other blues

clear glue chip with dichroic coating or
   iridized clears

sandblasting resist*

craft knife and no. 11 blades

black acrylic paint

gold and silver metal leaf, adhesive size,
   and lacquer

silver chain

beads

thin gauge wire such as tinned copper**

heavier gauge wire to form hanger
   (optional)

*vinyl resist was used for this piece, but two
   thicknesses of self-adhesive paper will also work*

**used to solder around the perimeter of the
   piece and to form the hook ring and bead
   dangle ring; also used to make the jump ring*

Tools ▾

copperfoil pattern shears

glass cutter

breaking pliers

needle nose pliers

grinder with 1/8-inch-diameter (.5 cm) bit

soldering iron

small paintbrush

sandblasting equipment***

***blasting can be done at a stained glass studio,
   sign shop, or monument company*

Instructions ▾

1. Trace the pattern. Cut between the wings and the earth (the heavy dark line) with pattern shears.

2. Glue the pattern to the glass. Cut and grind the glass to the shape of the pattern. Soak the pattern off with water; clean and dry the glass.

3. Copperfoil the three pieces and solder them.

4. Run thin-gauge wire in the cold solder bead to tie the pieces together and help build up a heavier perimeter. Continue the wire along the solder line between the earth and the wing. By bending the wire sharply with needle nose pliers, the feather shapes can be further defined. Continue this to the top of the earth, and twist the wire to form the hook. Work down the other side in the same way. A second wire can be run from the bottom portion of the wings to the bottom of the earth for the chain and bead dangle.

5. Clean, patina, wash, and dry.

6. Apply resist to the front surface of the glass.

7. Transfer the feather design to the wings and continent shapes.

8. Cut the feather and continent outlines with the craft knife. Remove those portions of the resist to be blasted.

9. Cover the backs of these three pieces with self-adhesive paper or tape. Sandblast lightly (you are providing an outline for the imaging and a tooth for the base coat of paint and the metal leaf to cling to).

10. Remove the resist and clean the glass.

11. Paint the sandblasted areas with black paint (use the craft knife to scrape the paint off the nonblasted areas).

12. Apply leafing adhesive size with a small brush. Apply the metal leaf. Burnish the leaf and apply the lacquer.

13. Solder on the jump ring and silver chain. Hang the beads. Make a hook of heavy-gauge wire to use as a hanger.

Designer: Mary Jane Miller
Size: 5 inches (2 cm)

Tin Angel Ornaments

*Shiny tin angels are a welcome sight on any Christmas tree. Designed
by Mary Jane Miller, these companionable cherubs are easy to make.*

Materials ▾

10 x 12-inch (25.5 x 30.5 cm) piece of
    roofing tin or aluminum flashing
work gloves

Tools ▾

ball peen hammer

metal scribe or sharp nail

small metal shears

pounding board (plywood or rubber)

thin magazine

flat screwdriver

half-round file or medium-grit sandpaper

3/16-inch (8.5 cm) metal drill or nail

Instructions ▾

1. Sketch your angel figures on paper, then
trace the outlines. Cut out the angels with
metal shears. File or sand any sharp edges.

2. Using the photo as a guide, draw in the
detail lines with the metal scribe. Place the
angels on the pounding board and gently
hammer in these details with the tip of a
screwdriver. Angle the tip as you follow
the curves.

3. Place a magazine on the pounding
board. Turn the angels over and pound
out the beveled areas using the ball end of
the hammer to give form to the body and
wings.

4. Drill a hole at the top to attach a string
or wire, or hammer a hole through with a
nail and file the back edge until smooth.

Designer: Dana Irwin
Size: 22 inches long (56.5 cm)

Wire Angel

The inspiration for this distinctive angel designed by Dana Irwin is the popular Rockefeller Plaza version in New York City (pictured opposite). If you want yours to glow, simply wind tiny lights around the finished angel.

Materials ▾

dark grey steel wire, medium-gauge
heavy-gauge copper tubing
thin copper wire
2 x 2-foot (62 x 62 cm) plywood board,
 1/4-inch-thick (1 cm)
work gloves

Tools ▾

needle nose pliers
finishing nails
hammer

Instructions ▾

1. Draw your angel pattern on the plywood board at a diagonal angle to maximize the space. Hammer the nails in at each corner of the design and along the main lines and curves of the pattern.

2. Anchor the wire around the nail you choose as your starting point; then, wind the wire around and around the entire design, until you are satisfied with the thickness.

3. As reinforcement, bind multiple strands of wire at major points (i.e., where the pattern curves), so that when you lift the

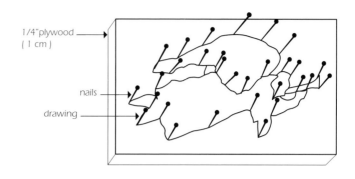

angel off the board, the angel will not collapse inward or flop over.

4. Shape the copper tubing into a halo and wire it on.

5. Use thin copper wire to fashion the hair. To obtain the curly locks pictured here, wind the wire around a pencil or dowel to the size of the desired curls and attach with steel wire.

6. Now's the time to add lights, if you so desire.

7. Suspend the angel with steel wire, attached at two points.

Note: You can make this angel any size you want. Make sure the board you buy will accommodate it.

Angelic Chorus

This beautiful trio of stained glass angels, designed by Don Wood, will add a lyrical touch to your home year 'round or during the Christmas season.

Designer: Don C. Wood

Size: 10 inches (25.5 cm), 7 inches 18 cm, and 5 inches (13 cm)

154
▼

Materials ▾

opaque glass for body in color of your choice

clear patterned glass for wings

white opaque glass for books

preformed glass gem for head (or use same glass as for wings)

16-gauge tin-plated copper wire for halos

lead came: 1/8 to 3/16-inch U (.5 cm) for body, head, and wings

lead came: 1/16 inch (0.5 cm) for arms and books

solder (50/50 of 60/40 solid core solder)

liquid soldering flux

felt tip pen or grease pencil

dish washing detergent

steel wool soap pads

glass cleaner

Tools ▾

glass cutter

glass breaking pliers

lead came knife

soldering iron

Instructions ▾

1. Trace the patterns on the glass. You will need two bodies, wings, and books per angel. Be sure to flip the body and wing patterns over to allow for left and right components. Use a glass gem for the head, or cut a circle of glass.

2. Wrap each component with the appropriate lead came. To facilitate soldering and hide the soldering joint, start the lead at the neck area of the body and the top of the wings.

3. Solder the two body segments together at right angles. You don't need to solder the entire length; just tack them together at the top and bottom. (The right angle is easily accomplished by using the edge of your worktable as a 90 degree jig.)

4. Position and tack solder each wing to the body, soldering just at the neck area. When viewed from above, the body segments and wings form an approximate x-shape.

5. Run a 1-1/2-inch (4 cm) decorative bead of solder from the neck down the front.

6. Assemble the two components of the book in a 90 degree angle and tack solder at the top and bottom.

7. Form a curved segment of came for the arms about 2 inches (5 cm) long. Position the arms and tack solder in position.

8. Position and solder the assembled books in place.

9. Position the lead-wrapped head and tack solder both the front and back.

10. Form the halo by twisting two segments of wire together and wrapping them around a medium-sized can about 3 inches (7.5 cm) in diameter. Position and tack solder the halo on the back side of the head.

11. Reinforce the entire angel by beading solder on the back side from the neck area down between the wings for about 1-1/2 inches (4 cm). Inspect the angel for any solder joints that need reinforcing or touching up.

12. Thoroughly clean the angel with dish washing detergent and steel wool pads. Spray with glass cleaner and dry with a soft towel.

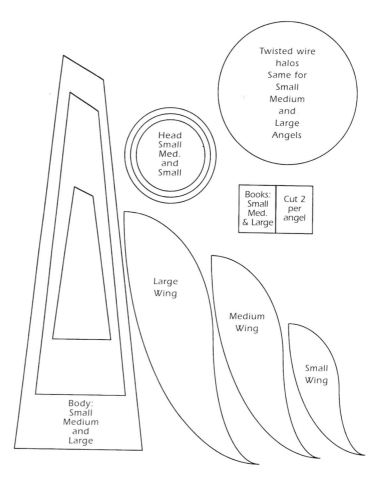

Twisted wire halos Same for Small Medium and Large Angels

Head Small Med. and Small

Books: Small Med. & Large   Cut 2 per angel

Large Wing

Medium Wing

Small Wing

Body: Small Medium and Large

Enlarge all 200%

Tin and Painted-Wood Angel

Designed by Mary Jane Miller and Valentin Gomez, this angel shimmers beautifully when light (moonlight or candlelight) dances across the wings and robe.

Designers: Mary Jane Miller and Valentin Gomez
Size: 8 x 15 inches (20 x 38.5 cm)

Materials ▾

1/2 x 12 x 18-inch (1.5 x 30.5 x 46 cm) plywood

1/8 x 2 x 3-inch (.5 x 5 x 7.5 cm) fiber-board

10 x 15-inch (25.5 x 38.5 cm) piece of roofing tin or aluminum flashing

latex house paint: flesh tones, dark brown, white, and rose

small book or other prop

small nails

small bolt or rivet and washer

work gloves

Tools ▾

jigsaw with fine scroll blade

small metal shears

metal scribe or sharp nail

large nail

corrugated cardboard

paintbrush

half-round file or medium-grit sandpaper

Instructions ▾

1. Draw the angel outline on plywood. Cut it out with the jigsaw and sand the edges smooth. The front arm is cut from 1/8-inch (.5 cm) fiberboard.

2. Place the plywood angel on the aluminum and trace a 1/4-inch (1 cm) margin all the way around it with a metal scribe. Cut this out with metal shears. Cut out two pieces of tin for the hair and one for the far wing. File or sand any sharp edges.

3. Place the aluminum angel on the cardboard and scribe the details of the robe, dress, hair, and wings with a large nail.

4. Turn the tin pieces over and scribe a parallel set of lines to create a raised pattern on the right side of the angel. The tip of the nail can be slightly rounded off with a file to prevent tearing the aluminum.

5. Paint the face, arms, and feet as you wish.

6. Nail the sections of aluminum onto the wood, with the two pieces of hair overlapping the wings. Hammer the 1/4-inch (1 cm) margins of aluminum around the edges of the wood. Drill a 1/4-inch (1 cm) hole in the shoulder of the front arm and attach it to the body with a small bolt or rivet and washer. Position the small book or prop in the front hand.

Enlarge 400%

▶ *Abou Ben Adhem (may his tribe increase!)*

Awoke one night from a deep dream of peace,

And saw, within the moonlight in his room,

Making it rich, and like a lily in bloom,

And angel writing in a book of gold:—

Exceeding peace had made Ben Adhem bold,

And to the presence in the room he said,

"What writest thou?" — The vision rais'd its head,

And with a look made of all sweet accord,

Answer'd, "The names of those who love the Lord."

"And is mine ont?" said Abou. "Nay, not so,"

Replied the angel. Abou spoke more low,

But cheerly still; and said, "I pray thee, then,

Write me as one that loves his fellow men."

The angel wrote, and vanish'd. The next night

It came again with a great wakening light,

And show'd the names whom love of God had blest,

And lo! Ben Adhem's name led all the rest.

LEIGH HUNT

Fear of Flying

Designer Trudel Terhune Gifford delights in celebrating what she sees as the humorous side of winged messengers. Faced with flying, her gentle, plump seraphim smiles apprehensively and catches hold of the wind, her wings shimmering with stars.

▶ ***Look***
homeward,
angel, now, and
melt with ruth.
JOHN MILTON
LYCIDAS

Designer: Trudel Terhune Gifford
Size: 6 x 7 inches (15.5 x 18 cm)

Materials ▾

10 x 10-inch (25.5 x 25.5 cm) piece of
    roofing tin (30-gauge terneplate*)

gold spray paint

small gold and silver star sequins

2 yards (2 m) 34-gauge brass wire

1/3 of a gold tinsel stem

2-ply gold or silver cord

steel wool

glue

masking tape

work gloves

**G-T Stained Glass and Tin Works, P.O. Box
7219, Albuquerque, New Mexico 87194, (505)
247-9322.*

Tools ▾

metal scribe

small metal shears

half-round file or medium-grit sandpaper

12 x 12-inch (31 x 31 cm) pounding board
    (steel or rubber)

thin (1/4-inch, 1 cm) magazine

thick (1/2-inch, 1.5 cm) magazine

ball peen hammer

stamps (for metal or leather): 3/8-inch
    (1.25 cm) crescent, 3/16-inch (.75 cm)
    crescent, 1/4-inch (1 cm) circle, 3/16-
    inch (.75 cm) straight, 3/4-inch (2 cm)
    straight

small and large nails with points filed flat

small, sharp nail

Instructions ▾

1. Trace the pattern on the tin with a metal
scribe and cut it out with metal shears.
Note—Cutting tips: Wear work gloves; tin
is sharp. For a smoother edge, do not lift
the blades from the tin with each cut, but
let the shears guide. Cut around intricate
spots, such as fingers, then go back and
snip out the excess tin from the most con-
venient angle. Snip a tiny bit of tin off any
sharp points.

2. Checking both sides of the cut angel,
file or sand any rough edges.

3. Using a thin magazine on the pounding
board, stamp the designs according to the
pattern with a ball peen hammer.

4. Steel-wool both sides.

5. With a thick magazine on the pounding

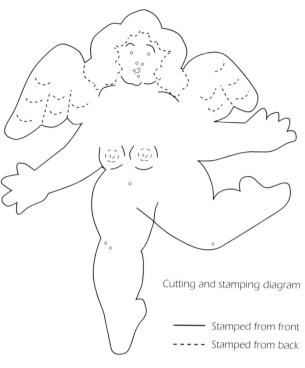

Cutting and stamping diagram

——— Stamped from front

- - - - Stamped from back

Enlarge 200%

board, punch a hole in the top of the
angel's head and punch four holes along
each wing/shoulder line. File the backs of
the holes smooth.

6. Spray paint the wings gold, first masking the rest of the angel. When dry, steel-
wool lightly, making the tin on the stamping visible.

7. Cut two 1-yard (1 m) pieces of brass
wire. Thread one piece through one of the
shoulder line holes and pull it through
halfway, with 18 inches (46 cm) extending
on each side of the hole. Taking one end,
wrap it around the wing and back through
a hole until you have gone through each of
the holes once. As you do this, add stars
wherever you like by threading them onto
the wire and then wrapping the wire
around the star and back through its hole to
anchor it. Do the same with the other 18-
inch (46 cm) piece of wire until there are
two wires through each hole. Wind the
ends of the wire around each other at the
top of the wing and twist a star onto the
wire at each end. Repeat for the other wing.

8. For hanging, half-hitch a double piece
of two-ply gold or silver cord through the
hole in the top of the head.

9. Twist one-third of a gold tinsel stem
into a halo and attach with glue.

Index

French Christmas Card, 1905.
Courtesy of E.T. Archive, London.